362
368
364

THE ENCYCLOPEDIA OF PSYCHOACTIVE DRUGS

SERIES 1

SERIES 2

DRUGS
&
CRIME

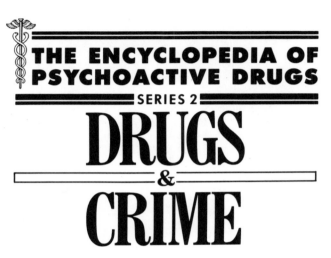

THE ENCYCLOPEDIA OF PSYCHOACTIVE DRUGS

SERIES 2

DRUGS & CRIME

THOMAS & DOROTHY HOOBLER

CHELSEA HOUSE PUBLISHERS

NEW YORK • PHILADELPHIA

EDITOR-IN-CHIEF: Nancy Toff
EXECUTIVE EDITOR: Remmel T. Nunn
MANAGING EDITOR: Karyn Gullen Browne
COPY CHIEF: Juliann Barbato
PICTURE EDITOR: Adrian G. Allen
ART DIRECTOR: Giannella Garrett
MANUFACTURING MANAGER: Gerald Levine

Staff for DRUGS AND CRIME

SENIOR EDITOR: Jane Larkin Crain
ASSOCIATE EDITOR: Paula Edelson
ASSISTANT EDITOR: Michele Merens
EDITORIAL ASSISTANT: Laura-Ann Dolce
COPY EDITOR: Terrance Dolan
ASSOCIATE PICTURE EDITOR: Juliette Dickstein
PICTURE RESEARCHER: Debra P. Hershkowitz
DESIGNER: Victoria Tomaselli
DESIGN ASSISTANT: Ghila Krajzman
PRODUCTION COORDINATOR: Joseph Romano
COVER PHOTO: James Colburn/Photo Reporters

CREATIVE DIRECTOR: Harold Steinberg

5   7   9   8   6   4

Library of Congress Cataloging in Publication Data

Hoobler, Thomas.
   Drugs & crime.
   (The Encyclopedia of psychoactive drugs. Series 2)
   Includes index.
   1. Narcotics and crime—Juvenile literature. 2. Narcotics,
Control of—Juvenile literature. 3. Drug abuse and crime—
Juvenile literature. I. Hoobler, Dorothy. II. Title. III. Title:
Drugs and crime. IV. Series.
HV5801.H64   1988   364.2   87–21826

ISBN 1-55546-228-6
     0-7910-0786-3 (pbk.)

CONTENTS

Any person who uses a drug forbidden by law is committing a crime. Even casual users of illicit substances become part of the international chain of criminal activity related to drugs.

In the Mainstream
of American Life

One of the legacies of the social upheaval of the 1960s is that psychoactive drugs have become part of the mainstream of American life. Schools, homes, and communities cannot be "drug proofed." There is a demand for drugs — and the supply is plentiful. Social norms have changed and drugs are not only available—they are everywhere.

But where efforts to curtail the supply of drugs and outlaw their use have had tragically limited effects on demand, it may be that education has begun to stem the rising tide of drug abuse among young people and adults alike.

Over the past 25 years, as drugs have become an increasingly routine facet of contemporary life, a great many teenagers have adopted the notion that drug taking was somehow a right or a privilege or a necessity. They have done so, however, without understanding the consequences of drug use during the crucial years of adolescence.

The teenage years are few in the total life cycle, but critical in the maturation process. During these years adolescents face the difficult tasks of discovering their identity, clarifying their sexual roles, asserting their independence, learning to cope with authority, and searching for goals that will give their lives meaning.

Drugs rob adolescents of precious time, stamina, and health. They interrupt critical learning processes, sometimes forever. Teenagers who use drugs are likely to withdraw increasingly into themselves, to "cop out" at just the time when they most need to reach out and experience the world.

A woman removes the seedpods from opium plants in Turkey. Until the early 1970s, much of the heroin that arrived in the United States originated in Turkish poppy fields.

Fortunately, as a recent Gallup poll shows, young people are beginning to realize this, too. They themselves label drugs their most important problem. In the last few years, moreover, the climate of tolerance and ignorance surrounding drugs has been changing.

Adolescents as well as adults are becoming aware of mounting evidence that every race, ethnic group, and class is vulnerable to drug dependency.

Recent publicity about the cost and failure of drug rehabilitation efforts; dangerous drug use among pilots, air traffic controllers, star athletes, and Hollywood celebrities; and drug-related accidents, suicides, and violent crime have focused the public's attention on the need to wage an all-out war on drug abuse before it seriously undermines the fabric of society itself.

The anti-drug message is getting stronger and there is evidence that the message is beginning to get through to adults and teenagers alike.

The Encyclopedia of Psychoactive Drugs hopes to play a part in the national campaign now under way to educate young people about drugs. Series 1 provides clear and comprehensive discussions of common psychoactive substances, outlines their psychological and physiological effects on the mind and body, explains how they "hook" the user, and separates fact from myth in the complex issue of drug abuse.

Whereas Series 1 focuses on specific drugs, such as nicotine or cocaine, Series 2 confronts a broad range of both social and physiological phenomena. Each volume addresses the ramifications of drug use and abuse on some aspect of human experience: social, familial, cultural, historical, and physical. Separate volumes explore questions about the effects of drugs on brain chemistry and unborn children; the use and abuse of painkillers; the relationship between drugs and sexual behavior, sports, and the arts; drugs and disease; the role of drugs in history; and the sophisticated drugs now being developed in the laboratory that will profoundly change the future.

Each book in the series is fully illustrated and is tailored to the needs and interests of young readers. The more adolescents know about drugs and their role in society, the less likely they are to misuse them.

Joann Rodgers
Senior Editorial Consultant

A one-time advocate of the therapeutic use of cocaine, Sigmund Freud would have been astounded had he known that this drug would one day fuel the most lucrative criminal empire of all time.

INTRODUCTION

The Gift of Wizardry
Use and Abuse

JACK H. MENDELSON, M.D.
NANCY K. MELLO, Ph.D.
Alcohol and Drug Abuse Research Center
Harvard Medical School—McLean Hospital

Dorothy to the Wizard:
"I think you are a very bad man," said Dorothy.
"Oh no, my dear; I'm really a very good man; but I'm a very bad Wizard."
—from THE WIZARD OF OZ

Man is endowed with the gift of wizardry, a talent for discovery and invention. The discovery and invention of substances that change the way we feel and behave are among man's special accomplishments, and, like so many other products of our wizardry, these substances have the capacity to harm as well as to help. Psychoactive drugs can cause profound changes in the chemistry of the brain and other vital organs, and although their legitimate use can relieve pain and cure disease, their abuse leads in a tragic number of cases to destruction.

Consider alcohol — available to all and yet regarded with intense ambivalence from biblical times to the present day. The use of alcoholic beverages dates back to our earliest ancestors. Alcohol use and misuse became associated with the worship of gods and demons. One of the most powerful Greek gods was Dionysus, lord of fruitfulness and god of wine. The Romans adopted Dionysus but changed his name to Bacchus. Festivals and holidays associated with Bacchus celebrated the harvest and the origins of life. Time has blurred the images of the Bacchanalian festival, but the theme of drunkenness as a major part of celebration has survived the pagan gods and remains a familiar part of modern society. The term "Bacchanalian Festival" conveys a more appealing image than "drunken orgy" or "pot party," but whatever the label, drinking alcohol is a form of drug use that results in addiction for millions.

The fact that many millions of other people can use alcohol in moderation does not mitigate the toll this drug takes on society as a whole. According to reliable estimates, one out of every ten Americans develops a serious alcohol-related problem sometime in his or her lifetime. In addition, automobile accidents caused by drunken drivers claim the lives of tens of thousands every year. Many of the victims are gifted young people, just starting out in adult life. Hospital emergency rooms abound with patients seeking help for al-cohol-related injuries.

Who is to blame? Can we blame the many manufacturers who produce such an amazing variety of alcoholic beverages? Should we blame the educators who fail to explain the perils of intoxication, or so exaggerate the dangers of drinking that no one could possibly believe them? Are friends to blame — those peers who urge others to "drink more and faster," or the macho types who stress the importance of being able to "hold your liquor"? Casting blame, however, is hardly con-structive, and pointing the finger is a fruitless way to deal with the problem. Alcoholism and drug abuse have few cul-prits but many victims. Accountability begins with each of us, every time we choose to use or misuse an intoxicating substance.

It is ironic that some of man's earliest medicines, derived from natural plant products, are used today to poison and to intoxicate. Relief from pain and suffering is one of society's many continuing goals. Over 3,000 years ago, the Therapeutic Papyrus of Thebes, one of our earliest written records, gave instructions for the use of opium in the treatment of pain. Opium, in the form of its major derivative, morphine, and similar compounds, such as heroin, have also been used by many to induce changes in mood and feeling. Another ex-ample of man's misuse of a natural substance is the coca leaf, which for centuries was used by the Indians of Peru to reduce fatigue and hunger. Its modern derivative, cocaine, has im-portant medical use as a local anesthetic. Unfortunately, its increasing abuse in the 1980s clearly has reached epidemic proportions.

The purpose of this series is to explore in depth the psychological and behavioral effects that psychoactive drugs have on the individual, and also, to investigate the ways in which drug use influences the legal, economic, cultural, and even moral aspects of societies. The information presented here (and in other books in this series) is based on many clinical and laboratory studies and other observations by people from diverse walks of life.

Over the centuries, novelists, poets, and dramatists have provided us with many insights into the sometimes seductive but ultimately problematic aspects of alcohol and drug use. Physicians, lawyers, biologists, psychologists, and social scientists have contributed to a better understanding of the causes and consequences of using these substances. The authors in this series have attempted to gather and condense all the latest information about drug use and abuse. They have also described the sometimes wide gaps in our knowledge and have suggested some new ways to answer many difficult questions.

One such question, for example, is how do alcohol and drug problems get started? And what is the best way to treat them when they do? Not too many years ago, alcoholics and drug abusers were regarded as evil, immoral, or both. It is now recognized that these persons suffer from very complicated diseases involving deep psychological and social problems. To understand how the disease begins and progresses, it is necessary to understand the nature of the substance, the behavior of addicts, and the characteristics of the society or culture in which they live.

Although many of the social environments we live in are very similar, some of the most subtle differences can strongly influence our thinking and behavior. Where we live, go to school and work, whom we discuss things with — all influence our opinions about drug use and misuse. Yet we also share certain commonly accepted beliefs that outweigh any differences in our attitudes. The authors in this series have tried to identify and discuss the central, most crucial issues concerning drug use and misuse.

Despite the increasing sophistication of the chemical substances we create in the laboratory, we have a long way to go in our efforts to make these powerful drugs work for us rather than against us.

The volumes in this series address a wide range of timely questions. What influence has drug use had on the arts? Why do so many of today's celebrities and star athletes use drugs, and what is being done to solve this problem? What is the relationship between drugs and crime? What is the physiological basis for the power drugs can hold over us? These are but a few of the issues explored in this far-ranging series.

Educating people about the dangers of drugs can go a long way toward minimizing the desperate consequences of substance abuse for individuals and society as a whole. Luckily, human beings have the resources to solve even the most serious problems that beset them, once they make the commitment to do so. As one keen and sensitive observer, Dr. Lewis Thomas, has said,

> There is nothing at all absurd about the human condition. We matter. It seems to me a good guess, hazarded by a good many people who have thought about it, that we may be engaged in the formation of something like a mind for the life of this planet. If this is so, we are still at the most primitive stage, still fumbling with language and thinking, but infinitely capacitated for the future. Looked at this way, it is remarkable that we've come as far as we have in so short a period, really no time at all as geologists measure time. We are the newest, youngest, and the brightest thing around.

DRUGS
&
CRIME

New York City police commissioner Benjamin Ward bluntly states that "I believe the crime problem in America today is the drug problem."

AUTHOR'S PREFACE

The international drug trade is one of the world's largest business enterprises. A chain of drug dealers and their connections extends around the world, linking together an Indian coca planter living in the Andes Mountains, a cocaine-sniffing rock star in the United States, an opium farmer in Burma, and the heroin addict in Amsterdam. There are many middlemen along the way who cut a slice of the fabulous profits for themselves.

The manufacture, sale, and purchase of such drugs as heroin, cocaine, and marijuana are illegal in the United States and most of the world. The very illegality of these drugs is what makes them valuable products, for people must pay more to buy what the law forbids. Furthermore, the drug business is connected to a host of other crimes — murder, bribery, smuggling, and bank fraud among them. Illegalities that revolve around the buying and selling of illicit drugs constitute much of the criminality of our time.

The consumption of illegal drugs is much higher in the United States than in any other industrialized country; consequently, the crime problem is greatest there. "I believe the crime problem in America today *is* the drug problem," says New York City's police commissioner Benjamin Ward.

James D. Harmon, Jr., chief counsel for the President's Commission on Organized Crime, displays a sawed-off shotgun at a hearing on heroin trafficking. Such weapons are routine tools of the drug trade.

Every American who uses a drug forbidden by law is committing a crime. Despite this fact, there has been a huge rise in incidences of illegal drug use since the 1960s and a corresponding rise in the number of Americans arrested for drug crimes. Studies have shown that many Americans simply do not regard their drug use as criminal behavior. In fact, even the casual drug user becomes part of the worldwide chain of criminal activity related to drugs.

Widespread drug use has created a market for illicit substances that is largely controlled by organized crime. In 1986, the President's Commission on Organized Crime stated: "Drug trafficking is the single most serious organized crime problem in the world today." The drug trade is alluring to criminals because the profits are so fantastic. At the very least, tens of billions of dollars are channeled into the drug trade every year. Criminals engaged in this business at all levels are willing to commit any crime to keep control of the trade and these profits. Murder and corruption of law enforcement and government officials at all levels are routine by-products of the drug trade. The vast wealth of some drug traders has given them power to corrupt whole countries.

Tremendous profits are made possible for various reasons. Since some drugs are illegal and difficult to obtain, practically any price can be charged for them. The cost of these drugs in the legal market would be only a small fraction of the price they can command as illegal substances.

For example, marijuana, aptly called "weed," will grow anywhere with little cultivation. Yet adults, teenagers, and

Twenty million dollars worth of cocaine, almost a half million dollars in cash, and various weapons were seized by Los Angeles narcotics officers in a series of raids in just one night in 1982.

even preteens spend millions of dollars each year on bags of marijuana obtained illegally. The coca plant grows wild throughout the Andean region. It costs little to process the plant and extract cocaine from its leaves, buds, and stem. Yet, people pay up to $1,000 and more an ounce for cocaine once it has been diluted.

Another reason for drugs' high profitability is that there is a strong demand for them. In 1985, there were 800,000 arrests in the United States for drug violations — double the figure for 1970. The number of Americans who have used marijuana is estimated to be somewhere between 20 million and 40 million.

Though the figures for heroin and cocaine users are much smaller, sales of these drugs also reap billions of dollars in profits for dealers. Heroin and cocaine are physically or psychologically addictive for many people. Once "hooked," users of these drugs will pay any price to support their habit, whatever the cost to them or their families. Because the drugs can be quite expensive, some users will turn to street crimes such as robbery and burglary for money. In neighborhoods where the incidences of drug use and sales are high, everyday life is often marred by fear and violence. The resources of the police and the justice system in America have been strained by the growing problem of drugs. No one can measure the cost to society of crimes caused by drugs.

Certainly, the drug problem is not confined to the United States. Industrialized countries such as Canada, Japan, and the nations of Europe have acknowledged an increasing demand for drugs among their citizenry. The Soviet Union recently admitted that there is a drug problem in that country. However, the scale of drug use in other developed countries is still less than it is in the United States.

In some underdeveloped countries, drug use is an accepted part of the culture. It is primarily underdeveloped nations in South America and Asia that produce such drug crops as opium, coca leaves, and marijuana. Increasing use of these drugs in the United States has created a huge market in export trade for these countries.

On the other hand, drug production has, in some instances, distorted normal patterns of economic growth and prevented the development of standard agricultural products

22

or industries in these nations. Because the drug trade is so lucrative and is always involved with criminal activity, nations producing drugs or crops that can be processed into drugs have been besieged by corruption and violence. Drug traffickers have, in some cases, brought down national governments and worked with guerrilla revolutionary movements. Consequently, despite the allure of profits, no nation has truly profited from producing drugs.

Barrels of illicit beer are destroyed during Prohibition. The 18th Amendment resulted not in nationwide abstinence but in enormous profits for those involved in the illicit manufacture of alcohol.

CHAPTER 1

A HISTORICAL VIEW OF DRUGS AND CRIME

Since ancient times, people have used marijuana, opium (from which heroin is derived), and coca leaves. These drugs were consumed for both medicinal and mood-altering purposes in the regions in which they were grown.

The first Western reference to a connection between drugs and crime came when Marco Polo returned to Europe from his travels in the Far East. Polo told the tale of the Man of the Mountains, who lived on what is today the Iran-Iraq border. From his mountain stronghold, he sent out henchmen to kill his enemies. The Old Man secured the loyalty of his bloody band of terrorists by keeping them well supplied with a drug that was probably hashish, a concentrated form of marijuana. His followers were known as the Assassins, a form of the word hashish.

When Drugs Were Legal

Drug use was not illegal in the United States during the 19th century. Because many psychoactive drugs were derived from various plants that were not indigenous to the United States, they were not commonly used. Drugs were taken, when they were taken at all, for medicinal purposes. Initial

An ancient Greek relief carving depicts wheat and poppy plants. Opiates, which are derived from the poppy, have been consumed for medicinal and mood-altering purposes for thousands of years.

problems with addiction emerged during the Civil War. Throughout that conflict, doctors eased the pain of wounded soldiers with morphine, a derivative of opium. Because many veterans became addicted to morphine, addiction to this drug became known as the soldier's disease.

Opium use for nonmedicinal purposes was introduced by Chinese immigrants, who started coming to the United States in the middle of the 19th century. This practice remained restricted for a time to the Chinese community. In the post–Civil War period, however, opium became more widely used and opium-based products were prescribed for all kinds of ailments. Heroin, an opium derivative, was introduced at the turn of the century and was sold in drugstores and through the mail. It was marketed by the Bayer Company as a cure for morphine addiction and as a cough medicine and cure-all for such ailments as the common cold.

Cocaine, introduced in the 1880s, was also heralded by doctors as a cure for many illnesses. Both heroin and cocaine were prescribed for asthma, fatigue, nausea, and other conditions. The founder of psychoanalysis, Sigmund Freud, initially believed that cocaine was a useful drug for treating depression.

In the last 20 years of the 19th century, patent medicines did not have to be licensed and were sold over the counter. But these concoctions often contained ingredients that would be regarded as dangerous today. The Parke-Davis Company marketed a cocaine cigar that "cured the blues." Teas, candies, and lozenges containing cocaine were widely sold. A product known as Vin Mariani, a mixture of cocaine and wine, had a devoted following among such diverse people as Ulysses Grant, Thomas Edison, and Pope Leo XIII. The original Coca-Cola, introduced in 1885 as a patent medicine "tonic," was liberally laced with cocaine.

By the end of the 19th century, abuse of the opiates found in patent medicines had reached epidemic proportions. People started to reconsider their unthinking reliance on various "medicinal" concoctions. Heroin was reexamined by scientists, doctors, and researchers and found to be even more addictive than morphine. There were reports that cocaine had produced disturbing side effects and addiction among some users, including hallucinations, irrational behavior, and changes in personality. In 1903, the Coca-Cola Company dropped cocaine from its formula.

A medieval miniature depicts Marco Polo and his brother leaving the court of Kublai Khan. Polo returned to Europe with tales of the Man of the Mountains, an outlaw who plied his followers with hashish.

Unfortunately, not all of this emerging antidrug sentiment was just or rational, and much of it was tainted by racist stereotyping and hysteria. For example, in 1910, a federal survey claimed "cocaine is often the direct incentive to the crime of rape by the Negroes in the South and other sections of the country." Some southern law-enforcement officials claimed that blacks under the influence of cocaine became criminals with superhuman powers. Another minority group, the Chinese, were blamed for spreading addiction to opium. Partly out of a genuine concern over the effects of certain drugs, partly out of ignorance and prejudice, the public mood began to move inexorably toward the cause of prohibition.

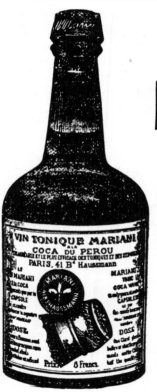

In the late 19th century the dangers of cocaine and heroin were not yet known. Both were advertised as potent pain relievers, and both were active ingredients in various medicines sold over the counter.

Opium is boiled and tested in this engraving from the 1880s. Importation of this drug, which was first brought to the United States by Chinese immigrants in the 1850s, was outlawed in 1909.

The Move for Prohibition

In 1903, the International Opium Commission met in Shanghai, China. Representatives from 12 countries called for joint action against the growing misuse of drugs. At the Hague Conference in 1912, the major nations of the world agreed to restrict the production and trade in opiates to the amount needed for medicinal supplies.

Domestically, the U.S. government began to take action too. The Pure Food and Drug Act of 1906 required labels on all medicines to state clearly the alcohol, narcotic (heroin and all derivatives of opium), and cocaine contents. Two years later, an amendment to that bill prohibited the shipping of alcohol, heroin, and cocaine across state lines. Many states passed laws regulating the sale and use of cocaine, and the federal government outlawed the import of opium in 1909.

In 1914, Congress passed the Harrison Narcotics Act. This law required anyone who imported, manufactured, or sold narcotics (cocaine was mislabeled as a narcotic) to register with the government and pay a special tax. The Treasury Department was charged with enforcing the law. Even so, doctors in clinics designed to treat addicts could freely dispense the drug. After a court case in the 1920s, however, these restrictions became virtual bans. Doctors were no longer allowed to dispense drugs to addicts even under controlled situations, and the possession of drugs by an addict became illegal. In 1924 Congress prohibited the manufacture of heroin in the United States for any purpose. Drug use ceased to be a medical problem and became instead a law enforcement problem.

In the 1920s and 1930s marijuana made its appearance on the American scene. Initially it was brought to the United States in significant quantities by Mexican immigrants who came into the country in search of jobs. Marijuana was regarded with horror by the vast majority of the population, however, as can be seen in the 1936 film *Reefer Madness*, which portrayed the marijuana smoker as a dangerous and uncontrollable lunatic.

Harry Anslinger (right), first head of the Federal Bureau of Narcotics, celebrates the passage of antidrug legislation in 1956.

In 1932, a Federal Bureau of Narcotics was created within the Treasury Department to enforce the antidrug laws in this country. Harry Anslinger was head of the Bureau from its inception until the 1950s. Anslinger was critically influential in forming the general public's impression of marijuana in the period spanning these two decades. He led an effective campaign against the "killer weed," the use of which he claimed led to criminal behavior and to experimentation with more dangerous drugs. Largely through his efforts, a federal law prohibiting marijuana was passed in 1937.

Anslinger also fought all attempts to classify drug addicts as people needing medical help. He was virulently opposed to the legalization of drug use under medical supervision. The only concession the Bureau made for drug users was the establishment of a hospital at Lexington, Kentucky, where addicts could go to be detoxified.

Organized Crime and Drugs

Like other drugs, alcohol became a target of federal legislation in the early 1900s. The 18th Amendment to the U.S. Constitution, which prohibited the manufacture and sale of alcoholic beverages, was ratified in 1919. This amendment failed to deter Americans from their drinking habits, however. Its major effect, unforeseen at the time, was to increase the possible profits for those who imported, made, or sold alcoholic beverages. Criminals in the United States organized to take advantage of Prohibition and consequently the Mafia, with its local "families" throughout the country, increased in power. A Mafia member, Salvatore Lucania, more commonly known as Lucky Luciano, realized that criminals had much to gain by cooperating with each other. In 1931 he organized the Commission, a loose federation that made decisions in matters that could affect relations among the Mafia families. The families grew rich and powerful through their involvement in the smuggling and sale of alcoholic beverages.

With repeal of Prohibition in 1933, a significant source of organized crime's income was cut off. Luciano saw future possibilities in drugs as the replacement for alcohol. The draconian policies of Harry Ans' ger had not succeeded in stamping out drug use. There were still people who wanted illegal drugs and, as with alcohol, Luciano organized criminals

Lucky Luciano leaves court in 1936. Despite the fact that Luciano was arrested 25 times, he was a kingpin in the illegal drug trade from the time of Prohibition to his death in 1962.

to service their needs. He directed the importation of heroin and set up a distribution system for the drug within the United States. Luciano remained important in the drug trade until his death in 1962.

Drug Use Increases

Drug use dropped sharply during World War II, and during the postwar period remained largely confined to urban ghettos and among groups, such as jazz musicians, who were well out of the mainstream. Nonetheless, despite new legislation that had toughened penalties for trafficking in drugs, rates of abuse began to climb again in the early 1950s. With the emergence of the beat generation, drug use again broke into the consciousness of the nation. Rebels against conformity and middle-class values, the "beats" made drugs a symbol of their intellectual and moral alienation from society. But the number of beatniks was small.

Marijuana use first became popular among a broader spectrum of Americans in the 1960s, a decade marked by intense cultural and political upheaval. Ordinary Americans, particularly the young, went into the streets to protest against the war in Vietnam and to support the civil rights movement. For the first time, many middle-class Americans found themselves in active opposition to the government's official policies. Taking their cue from the beats, college students also began to smoke pot as a way to distinguish themselves from the bourgeois society they disdained. Furthermore, they found that much of the propaganda about marijuana was exaggerated. "When people found out that marijuana didn't drive you wild and mad, the government lost what little credibility it had," said one commentator.

Charlie "Bird" Parker performing with trumpeter Miles Davis in 1947. One of the greatest saxophonists of all time, Parker was addicted to both alcohol and heroin and died in 1955 at the age of 35.

Accordingly, warnings about the dangers of marijuana and other drugs were ignored. A Harvard professor, Timothy Leary, became a public advocate of LSD, a hallucinogenic drug. His slogan, "turn on, tune in, drop out," became a rallying cry for a generation of disaffected young people. The sale and possession of all kinds of illegal drugs increased significantly and became socially acceptable in many places. The warning that marijuana use "could lead to harder stuff" seemed confirmed by the fact that heroin use soared in places like the Haight-Ashbury section of San Francisco, a gathering place for young people who had dropped out from society.

Although the dark side of drug addiction was recognized by the end of the 1960s, drug use had become deeply embedded in American society by that time. Synthetic drugs, such as phencyclidine (PCP or "angel dust"), methamphetamine, and quaaludes, became increasingly popular. Many users indulged in multiple drug use. In addition, some veterans of the Vietnam War became heroin addicts while in the service and brought this dependency back to the United States.

In 1970, Congress passed the Controlled Substances Act, which made possession of small quantities of marijuana a misdemeanor, while the sale or transfer of the drug remained a felony.

During the 1970s, methadone maintenance programs were also introduced nationwide to provide heroin addicts with a substitute drug. Although methadone, like heroin, was addictive, it was administered under a doctor's supervision for a small fee or even dispensed free of charge under some programs. It was hoped that methadone maintenance would remove the addict from a life of crime, simply by making it unnecessary for him to commit crimes to finance his habit.

Needless to say, the heroin problem did not go away, but in the 1970s it was overshadowed by the reappearance of an epidemic abuse of cocaine. This drug seemed to fit the needs of the "me generation." Because of its high cost, it became a status drug, "the champagne of the drug world." Its illegal use became glamorized by celebrities of the entertainment and sports worlds. Cocaine abuse also spread among doctors, lawyers, and other young professionals. Many people in the "fast track" worlds of Wall Street and the computer business were users. Not only were these upwardly mobile

Employees of various Wall Street institutions are led off to jail after being charged with narcotics possession and distribution.

Americans using the drug but they were dealing it as well. As a cocaine pusher who worked in Silicon Valley said, "It was made to order. I had an instant clientele — hundreds of people who worked with me." Drug dealing and drug use became a consistent problem for Fortune 500 companies, the army, and in various white-collar professions.

Cocaine continued to be the drug of choice in the 1980s, and by that time, the demand for it had attracted a new group of criminals from South America, primarily Colombia, who controlled the trade to the United States. America's increasing use of cocaine meant enormous profits for those dealing in this illicit substance. To service the market of people who claimed to have used cocaine — 22 million in 1982, up from 15 million in 1979 — dealers poured quantities of the drug into the United States by air, sea, and land.

The Drug Enforcement Administration (DEA), formed in 1973 by combining former drug agencies in different U.S.

Vice-president George Bush, head of the Reagan administration's South Florida Task Force, takes a ride on a U.S. Customs Service antidrug-smuggling patrol boat. The task force was established in 1982.

cabinet departments, was the foremost government agency attempting to stem the flow of illegal substances, including cocaine, into the country in the 1980s. The DEA has offices in most of the countries producing illicit drugs. Although the agency is not authorized to make arrests in foreign countries, it can collect and share information with foreign government agencies and officials. It also trains foreign narcotics agents.

The U.S. Customs Service, the Coast Guard, and the Immigration and Naturalization Service, among others, were also recruited in the effort to control drug trafficking. By law, the president must periodically tell Congress which countries are working to eliminate the cultivation, processing, or transit of drugs across their borders in order for these nations to continue to receive foreign aid from the United States. Sometimes this policy has caused conflicts between drug enforcement efforts and the foreign policy aims of the United States.

The Reagan administration has increased federal funding spent on drug-related law enforcement. In 1982 the Administration set up the South Florida Task Force, headed by Vice-president George Bush, to fight the war against drugs. Headquartered in the area that had become the main entry point for illegal drugs coming into the United States, the South Florida Task Force employed high-tech gadgetry, AWAC-type aircraft, special radar balloons, and ultramodern electronic communications equipment to stop the flow of drugs into southern Florida.

In 1986, Congress enacted legislation that increased the amount of money spent on law enforcement and stiffened penalties for violators of narcotics laws. This legislation also authorized grants to the states over a three-year period to assist in the development of state drug-control and drug-education programs. The law also prohibited so-called designer drugs, chemical substances that mimic the effects of illegal drugs but were not previously illegal because they were slightly different in chemical composition. It is still too soon to know whether these measures will be effective.

It was revealed in 1987 that Mafia members distributed about $1.6 billion worth of heroin in the United States from 1979 to 1984 through pizza parlors such as the Al Dente in Queens, New York.

CHAPTER 2

THE HEROIN TRADE

Heroin is derived from the poppy flower, or *Papaver somniferum*, which grows in many areas of Asia and Europe as well as in Mexico. Opium is found in the seedpod of this flower. After the flower blooms and the leaves fall off, harvesters make a couple of horizontal slits in the seedpod with a knife. The residue scraped off is opium. Boiled down with the addition of chemicals, opium becomes morphine base. Further refining, done in a laboratory, produces heroin.

The French Connection

Until the early 1970s, much of the heroin that arrived in the United States originated in the poppy fields of Turkey. From there, smugglers moved the raw opium to the Turkish city of Istanbul, Aleppo, Syria, and Beirut, Lebanon by car, truck, bus, or camel. Here the opium bricks were reduced in bulk by converting them to a morphine base. From Middle Eastern cities, the morphine base was then moved by land or sea to Europe for conversion to heroin.

Most European laboratories that converted morphine base to heroin were in Marseilles, in the south of France. The second largest city in France, Marseilles is the main base of the French underworld, known as the *milieu*. The milieu is composed primarily of Corsicans. Over the years, because of poverty on their home island, thousands of Corsicans emigrated to Marseilles seeking a better life. Most became hardworking citizens, but some turned to a life of crime.

Corsicans controlled the laboratories in Marseilles where morphine base was processed into heroin. Indeed, the heroin produced here was of the highest quality — it was called the "champagne of heroin." Members of the Marseilles milieu also served as middlemen between the countries producing opium bricks or morphine bases and organized crime elements, primarily the Mafia, involved in distributing heroin in the United States.

From Marseilles, the heroin was hidden in secret compartments of suitcases and smuggled into the United States by boat and airplane. Quantities of the drug also were strapped to the bodies of passengers, or hidden in automobiles. A famous case that inspired the movie *The French Connection* involved just such an automobile, brought to the United States by a popular French television star. Inside the car, a cache of over 150 pounds of heroin was hidden. Alert detective work by the New York City police resulted in the confiscation of the heroin and capture of some New York Mafia members in 1962, although several of the Corsicans involved in the caper escaped.

Marseilles was not the only base for Corsican operations. Auguste Ricord fled to Argentina from France after World War II to escape a death sentence for wartime collaboration with the Nazis. He developed a South American connection for heroin in the 1960s. In this operation, the heroin was shipped from France to Buenos Aires and other South American cities. Then it was smuggled into the United States via couriers, known as "mules." Large shipments of heroin were secreted in scientific instruments and other cargo, or flown directly to the United States by private plane. Often the pilots were professional smugglers known as *contrabandistas*. Previously they had smuggled consumer goods into South American countries to avoid high tariffs and returned to the United States empty-handed. Now they had a return cargo.

The French Connection was smashed in the 1970s when President Richard Nixon put diplomatic pressure on Turkey to stop the illegal planting and harvesting of poppies. Today, Turkey produces opium only for the legal medicinal market, but the country remains important as a transit center for drugs. The French government also closed secret heroin laboratories in its country, partly at the urging of the United States, but also because rates of heroin use had begun to rise in France.

Auguste Ricord, one of the most important heroin traders that the U.S. government has ever apprehended, arrived in the United States from Paraguay to face narcotics smuggling charges in 1972.

In addition, U.S. law-enforcement officials targeted Ricord. In 1972, he was extradited from Paraguay to the United States for trial. Ricord has turned out to be the most important heroin trader that the U.S. government has ever apprehended.

The Golden Triangle

With Turkey no longer producing opium poppies, three other areas of supply opened up. Today, they provide the major sources of heroin sold in the United States.

The first of these is the Golden Triangle — a region of Southeast Asia where Burma, Laos, and Thailand intersect. The legal governments of the three countries that merge in the Triangle lack control over the outlying mountain areas where opium is grown. In fact, these areas are home to ethnic tribes and rebel movements, some of which have their own private armies. Opium provides a source of cash for local warlords far greater than any other crop could. Frequently, the warlords have fought among themselves for control of

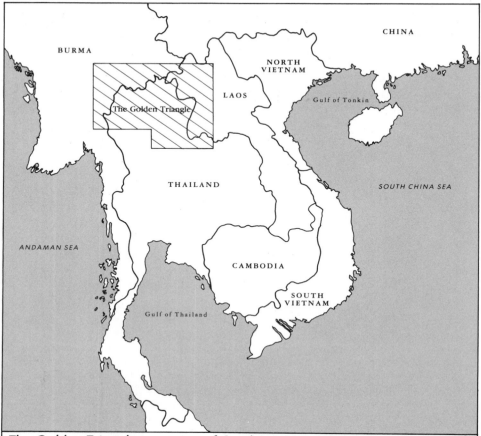

The Golden Triangle, a region of Southeast Asia where Laos, Burma, and Thailand meet, is a major source of heroin sold in the United States.

the opium. Currently, the leading opium warlord is Khun Sa, who commands the Shan State Army, a guerrilla band of several thousand troops that is ostensibly striving for independence from Burma.

Ten years ago, the king of Thailand made a serious effort to get the mountain people of his country to plant crops other than opium. The program reduced Thailand's opium production from over 100 tons a year to less than 20 tons in 1986. In March 1987, Thai government soldiers conducted a major offensive against Khun Sa's forces, some of whom operated in Thailand. Khun Sa, however, retreated into Burma, a country that was the world's largest producer of opium in 1987 despite various government eradication programs. As one Thai official said to the *Washington Post* in 1987, "Khun Sa is not going to get out of the drug business."

From the mountains of Southeast Asia, the opium is transported to Chiang Mai, a city in northern Thailand that is the center of the Golden Triangle trade. Here, the opium is processed into morphine base or heroin and then moved to Thailand's coastal regions.

Much of the Golden Triangle trade that still exists in Thailand is controlled by ethnic Chinese who emigrated to the country after the Chinese Civil War in 1948. The drug shipments go from Thailand to Hong Kong or Singapore for further processing or on to Europe.

The Golden Triangle heroin became important to Americans during the Vietnam War. Some veterans became rich as middlemen dealing in the heroin trade of this region. On a more tragic note, many American fighting men became addicted to heroin because it was so readily available in Southeast Asia.

A U.S. soldier in Vietnam buys drugs from a Vietnamese woman and youth in 1971. Heroin and other drugs were readily available to G.I.'s serving in the Vietnam War, and many of them returned home addicted.

The Golden Crescent

Most of the heroin sold in the United States comes from the Golden Crescent area, the region where Pakistan, Iran, and Afghanistan adjoin. As in the Golden Triangle, the opium-growing areas in these three nations are often not under the control of their respective governments.

Much of the opium produced in the Golden Crescent is consumed in the area itself. Iran has one of the worst heroin problems in the world. Estimates of the number of addicts in Iran range from 500,000 to 2 million. In contrast, the United States, with a population almost seven times that of Iran's, has about 500,000 addicts. Under the Khomeini regime, Iran has decreed the death penalty for users and traders. However, ongoing chaos in the country since the revolution in the 1980s has made efforts to stamp out the illicit trade increasingly difficult.

Afghanistan has also been in turmoil since the Soviet Union's invasion of that country in 1979. It appears that many Russian soldiers in Afghanistan have become addicted to heroin and are suffering a plight similar to that of the U.S. Vietnam War veterans who were exposed to and subsequently became addicted to this drug. However, some experts say that the Soviet Union has encouraged production.

In Pakistan, the poppy-growing areas are in the Northwest Provinces, inhabited by the Pathans, a minority ethnic group. The central Pakistani government controls the roads that run through the area but otherwise has little influence there. The Golden Crescent drug trade is centered in this region's city of Landi Kotal. There, one can openly buy drugs in any form.

The Pakistani government has made efforts to curtail drug trade within its borders because it is faced with a burgeoning addict population. However, in December 1986, Pathans went on a rampage in Karachi, Pakistan's largest city, killing at least 160 people and wounding hundreds more. Observers said the Pathans were angered by a police search of their neighborhoods for illegal drugs and arms. The government blamed drug dealers for inciting the riots.

From the Golden Crescent, heroin or morphine base is shipped to Europe. Frequently, this cargo is taken overland to Turkey, and from there moved by automobile across Europe. Turks, who are "guest workers" in European countries, are often recruited to drive these cars. The volume of traffic on European highways makes it impossible for law-enforcement officials to stop and search all cars.

Some countries are more responsible than others about checking for drugs at the border. Bulgaria, Turkey's neighbor, for example, has been regarded as very lax in attempting to halt the flow of drugs — to the point where some people believe that its officials participated in a guns-for-drugs trade. On the other hand, Yugoslavian authorities have a good reputation for being tough on drug traffickers.

After the breakup of the French Connection, Italy became the final European destination for morphine base. Heroin labs moved to Sicily and other parts of Italy. Often, some of the French Connection chemists moved with them. In Italy, the drug comes under the control of the Sicilian Mafia, and it is then smuggled into the United States.

The Mafia-controlled drug trade has spawned an epidemic of violence and murder in Italy. In 1984, these demonstrators marched in Rome to protest Mafia violence and raise public awareness of the problem.

The drug trade brought violence to Sicily in the late 1970s and early 1980s. In 1982 there were 151 Mafia-related killings in Palermo alone. While most of the victims of the drug wars were gang members, they also included the president of Sicily's regional government, Palermo's chief prosecutor, investigating magistrates, the provincial secretary of the Christian Democratic Party, and the regional chairmen of the Communist Party.

In 1982 the Italian government appointed General Carlo Alberto Della Chiesa — a man who had scored a number of victories against the terrorist Red Brigades — as head of a drive to stamp out the Mafia in Sicily. In September of that year, he was gunned down in the center of Palermo at the height of the rush hour. Although there were many witnesses, for months no one stepped forward. Every attorney in the Palermo prosecutor's office was protected by a 24-hour guard during that time. Finally, Sicilian workers held a general strike to protest Mafia violence and arouse public awareness. General Della Chiesa's successor arrested 500 Mafiosi, charging them with a broad range of crimes, including heroin trafficking. Many people brought to trial were convicted, and tough new laws were passed to enable prosecutors to get at the assets of the Mafia.

Mexican Heroin

Mexico is the third major source of heroin for the United States. Mexican heroin is produced in several provinces, including Sinaloa, Guerrero, Durango, and Chihuahua, and is processed within the country. The Mexican government has an eradication program, but it has only been sporadically successful. In 1986, poppy production in this country grew by 25%.

Because of Mexico's location, transportation of the drug to the United States is not a great problem. Some quantities are simply carried across the border by illegal aliens. Smugglers on planes and boats must only make a short trip to bring their cargoes into the United States. Much of the Mexican heroin is distributed to western and southwestern regions of the country. Chicago is another lucrative market for Mexican heroin. Though Mexico produces much less opium than countries in the Golden Crescent and the Golden Triangle,

U.S. customs officials display a cache of confiscated heroin that was being smuggled from Mexico in the backseat of an automobile.

the U.S. State Department revealed in 1987 that Mexico "is the primary single country supplier of heroin and marijuana to the United States."

The Pizza Connection

The 1986-87 trial of accused Mafia members in the "Pizza Connection" demonstrated that the Mafia's role in the heroin trade remains significant. Mafia members from Sicily came to the United States and set up pizzerias throughout the eastern half of the country. Approximately $1.6 billion worth of heroin was distributed within the United States from 1979 to 1984 through these pizza parlors. The heroin, government prosecutors charged, originated in Turkey as morphine base. The base was processed into heroin in Sicily and shipped to New York and other cities. Suitcases full of cash from the operation were "laundered" through banks and stockbrokers and transferred to overseas accounts. (For more details on the laundering of drug profits, see Chapter 5.)

Of the 22 original defendants in the case, two pleaded guilty, one was murdered, and another was seriously wounded on a New York street during the course of a turbulent trial. One juror was excused when her family received telephone threats. The court case took almost 16 months and cost the U.S. government several million dollars, but at its conclusion, 17 defendants were found guilty and faced long prison terms. One of the men convicted was said to have been the head of the Sicilian Mafia.

Rudolph Giuliani, the United States attorney in Manhattan, pointed to the government's success in putting the Mafia on trial for its crimes and declared, "If we continue our efforts, there's not going to be a Mafia in 5 to 10 years." Yet that would not mean the end of the drug trade. Giuliani claimed that the Mafia has lost part of the trade, but other organized criminal groups — Chinese, Vietnamese, Israeli, and Nigerian — are becoming increasingly important in the heroin industry, vying to take the Mafia's place.

Street Trade in Heroin

In the 1970s, some black dealers in the United States built important distribution networks of their own. The two most notable were Frank Matthews and Leroy ("Nicky") Barnes. Matthews in his heyday probably handled more heroin than any other single dealer. He had his own South American connection to import the drug directly. After being targeted for investigation, he was arrested, but after release on bail, he disappeared. One of the biggest manhunts in U.S. history was launched to find him, but he is still at large today.

The career of Nicky Barnes seemed to be a criminal success story. He began as a poor boy in Harlem, seemingly headed for a short, futile life when he became an addict as a young teenager. But he kicked his habit and became a street seller of heroin. On one of his brief stays in jail, he linked up with a big-time Mafia leader. After they were out of jail, the Mafia chieftain allowed Barnes to buy large quantities of the drug at relatively low prices. Barnes developed his own organization and soon became one of New York's most important drug dealers. He lived a lavish, public life style, flaunting his wealth and becoming a legend. Because he was careful not to touch heroin directly, he seemed to be immune from prosecution, but he was brought down at the end of the 1970s. Under New York's severe drug laws, he was sentenced to a long term in prison, where he remains.

To avoid criminal prosecution, the major importers of heroin try to get rid of the drug quickly after it comes to this country. A shipment is broken up and sold to smaller organizations or individual dealers on the street level. The people at the top of the trade remain as isolated as possible from the ultimate consumer. Indeed, in the drug trade, most people deal only with the person above them and know nothing about the organization other than their own job. This secrecy protects the security of the entire organization.

When heroin is first brought into the United States, it is usually at least 90% pure. It is then cut several times by middlemen. At each stage of distribution, the profit multiplies as the drug is cut and its price is increased. By the time it reaches street level, the substance is about 6% pure. The amount of opium sold by the grower for $1,000 is worth several million dollars by the time it is sold on the street.

In large cities, such as New York, which has half of the heroin addicts in the United States, the street trade in drugs is visible. People often accuse the police of laxity in enforcing drug laws. But in fact, the urban drug trade is so widespread that it would be beyond the resources of the police to apprehend and bring to trial all street dealers. Furthermore, because the trade is lucrative, arrested dealers would swiftly be replaced by others eager to take their places. Instead of pursuing street dealers, police have concentrated on infiltrating organizations that deal in large amounts of drugs. Often, they use street dealers as informants. This brings the police into contact with the drug trade in a way that has sometimes led to corruption. The connection between drugs and corruption of public officials will be further discussed in Chapter 6.

Workers in Colombia transform coca leaves into paste. A handful of South Americans have made billions of dollars acting as middlemen between the growers of the coca plant and U.S. dealers.

CHAPTER 3

THE COCAINE TRADE

In the 1970s and 1980s, cocaine use ballooned in the United States. Because of its high cost, its false reputation for being nonaddictive, and the fact that it was usually sniffed, rather than injected, cocaine attracted a different kind of user. Heroin had always been mainly a problem of the ghetto; its sale was associated with hardcore criminals; and its debilitating properties had earned it a bad reputation among casual drug users. But cocaine's popularity as a euphoric drug without apparent negative side effects quickly spread from rock stars — who sang thinly disguised lyrics about its virtues — to other figures in the entertainment world, sports heroes, and some of the idle rich who sought out the latest in expensive thrills.

Otherwise law-abiding citizens who traveled regularly to South America found that they could make enormous profits by carrying a relatively small quantity of cocaine back to the United States for resale. But the day of the amateur cocaine smuggler was shortlived. By the 1980s a cartel of Colombian families established control of the rapidly growing trade, and made billions of dollars in the process.

A dramatization of a businessman snorting cocaine illustrates the fact that use of this drug is very much a white-collar crime.

Sources of Cocaine

The coca bush, *Erythroxylon coca*, grows primarily in the Andes Mountains of Peru and Bolivia. Once the Colombian cartel seized control of the cocaine trade, the coca plant began to be cultivated in Colombia as well.

Traditionally, South American peasants have chewed the leaves of the coca plant as a palliative for hunger and exhaustion. Bazuco, a mixture of coca base and tobacco that is smoked, is widely used by young people in the slums of Colombia.

The coca bush grows rapidly. After three years, it can be harvested and baled. Sometimes the coca leaves are dissolved in kerosene to make coca paste. This decreases the weight of the leaves by 90%. Then the coca — leaves or paste — goes to a drug distribution center, such as Tinga Linda in Peru or Santa Cruz in Bolivia. Because the coca bush, in contrast to opium poppies and marijuana plants, is not found throughout the world but only in one specific area, a handful of powerful and ruthless dealers were able to gain control of the trade. Several of the big cocaine traders come from the major growing countries. One frequently noted example is Roberto Suarez of Bolivia.

Suarez started out as a wealthy cattle rancher; once he got into the cocaine business, however, he soon gained notoriety as the biggest dealer in the country. He personally owns vast coca plantations in Bolivia and controls a significant portion of all the coca that is destined to reach the United States as cocaine.

Laboratory processing transforms coca leaves and paste into cocaine base and cocaine itself. Most coca is refined outside the producing countries. Suarez is believed to have gained his preeminence by acting as the major middleman between the growers of coca leaves and the dealers who processed them into cocaine. By conservative estimates

Roberto Suarez's vast and lavish estate includes a dirt airstrip. Suarez owns coca plantations in Bolivia and reputedly controls much of the coca that eventually reaches the United States as cocaine.

Suarez has made over $400 million a year in the trade. He owns a fleet of planes and controls whole areas of the eastern part of Bolivia.

Under increasing pressure from the United States to clamp down on the production and export of coca, the Bolivian government asked for U.S. military assistance. In the 1986 Operation Blast Furnace, U.S. military forces and DEA agents assisted Bolivian troops in conducting raids on cocaine laboratories. The campaign succeeded in temporarily shutting down cocaine refining in Bolivia.

In February 1987 Bolivian and U.S. officials agreed to continue cooperating in the area of narcotics control and, furthermore, to persuade Bolivian farmers to abandon coca-bush planting in favor of other crops. But a U.S. State Department report has since concluded that, "no real progress was made on eradication in 1986; future progress is dependent on . . . creating opportunities for alternative livelihood for the rural population."

In Peru, there is evidence that the ultraviolent Maoist Shining Path guerrillas use profits from cocaine sales to pay for weapons. When the Peruvian government, at the urging

Backed by a Bolivian military plane, U.S. troops prepare for an antidrug sweep in the Bolivian lowlands. Several Latin American governments have helped the United States wage a war against drugs.

Despite the efforts of Peruvian president Alan Garcia, his country remains the world's largest producer of cocaine.

of the United States, instituted a program to encourage farmers to plant crops other than coca bushes, the guerrillas urged the peasants not to cooperate. Faced with instability within the country's borders, the government dropped the program. According to the U.S. State Department, Peru remains the world's largest cultivator of coca, despite the antidrug efforts of Peruvian president Alan Garcia, who has worked to stamp out coca growing since he took office in 1985.

The Colombian Connection

Many of the labs for processing cocaine originally surfaced in Argentina, Chile, and Brazil. In the 1970s, Colombian criminals assumed a principal role in processing and distributing the drug on an international scale. Because Colombia has ports on both the Atlantic and Pacific oceans, the country's criminal elements found it easy to smuggle goods into the United States. The smugglers used various means to transport

U.S. Coast Guard officers unload duffel bags of cocaine that were spotted floating off the coast of Key Biscayne, Florida. About 1,600 pounds of cocaine were recovered in this operation.

the drug. The Colombian airline Avianca became a major carrier for cocaine. Hundreds of people served as mules, carrying cocaine into the United States or to a third location, such as Panama, the Caribbean Islands, or Mexico, from which it was reshipped to the United States. The mules were supplied with false passports and various devices to hide the cocaine inside suitcases or in export products. Some mules swallowed cocaine wrapped in rubber containers to be excreted in the United States. This was dangerous because if the rubber burst, the courier could die. Mules were also usually accompanied by "shotguns," people in the organization who watched to see that the cocaine got to its destination safely. There was no difficulty finding mules; the pay was good. Americans were among those who became willing traffickers of drugs for pay.

But as the popularity of cocaine increased, the mule system could not satisfy the demand. Fleets of private planes laden with drug shipments took off from small airfields in

Colombia and landed throughout the southern United States, primarily in southern Florida. Ships filled with cocaine traveled to just beyond the 12-mile limit of the United States. From this point these large "mother" vessels were off-loaded into smaller, faster "cigarette" boats for the trip to the United States. The destination of choice was usually somewhere along the southern coast of Florida, which, with its large number of bays, is impossible to patrol completely.

When the cocaine arrives in the United States, it is almost pure. Subsequently, it is cut to about 12% before it is sold at street level. The Colombians maintain control of the trade through the middleman level, that is, up until the time it is turned over to the people who cut it with additives. The Colombians never sell to the consumer, and if caught in the United States, they usually skip bail and leave for Colombia.

The Colombians are also the main suppliers of cocaine for Europe. Madrid is the main European port of entry for the drug, but many European countries reported a sharp rise in the use of cocaine in the late 1970s. Amounts of the drug seized by authorities in Europe quadrupled between 1977 and 1981.

The Trail of Violence in the United States

The Colombian cartel established links with trusted subordinates in the United States, primarily in Miami and New York, as middlemen for the trade. There is no part of the United States that is unaffected by the cocaine trade, but its greatest impact has undoubtedly been on southern Florida. It is estimated that up to 70% of America's supply of cocaine enters the United States through this region.

In Miami, Colombian gangsters killed their rivals — Cubans, Americans, and other Colombians — without mercy. In 1979 a machine-gun battle erupted on Florida's Turnpike, a major thoroughfare. Months later there was a shootout in the busy Dadeland Mall. Three gunmen in an armored van bearing the name "Happy Time Complete Party Supply" riddled a liquor store with bullets. Two Colombians were killed and two innocent bystanders were wounded. In the violence of the late 1970s, Dade County's morgue had to buy a refrigerated trailer to handle the overflow. Unlike the Mafia, whose "soldiers" only killed rival gang members, the Colombians

President Ronald Reagan with Colombian president Belisario Betancur at the White House. The Reagan administration has tried to enlist Betancur's support for a 1979 treaty that allows the United States to extradite and try Colombian violators of U.S. drug laws.

wiped out whole families — wives, children, and even baby-sitters. Dade County police estimated that over 250 people died in the "cocaine wars" between 1979 and 1982.

In Queens, New York, another center of Colombian drug traders in the United States, there have been similar crimes. In February 1982, a Colombian dealer, his wife, and their two infant children were killed in their Mercedes automobile on a major New York City highway. Police found 140 pounds of cocaine and nearly $1 million in cash in their apartment.

In February, 1987, the inventor of the fast cigarette speedboats used to carry cocaine ashore during drug runs was shot and killed. A Federal official said it was a "typical hit" carried out by "Colombian drug traffickers." Presumably, the motivation for the killing was that millionaire American Donald Aronow, inventor of the cigarette boat, had been supplying his boats to law enforcement officials. Previously, the Colombians' possession of the boats had enabled them to outrun the Customs Service and Coast Guard vessels.

The Medellin Cartel

The headquarters of the Colombian drug trade is Medellin, the second largest city in Colombia. Medellin is a violent place that has become wealthy through its connection with the cocaine trade. At one time, the city reported as many as 12 murders a day. The loose organization of about 20 Colombian crime families who control the trade is known as the Medellin Cartel. The members of this cartel are the most dangerous organized-crime group in the world today. The four most important figures of the cartel are reported to be Pablo Escobar, Jorge Ochoa, Jose Rodriguez Gacha, and — until his recent arrest—Carlos Lehder.

Intelligence reports have revealed that Escobar began his criminal career stealing tombstones but established a true name for himself in the cocaine industry. His wealth is figured in the billions of dollars — an estimate that makes him the world's richest criminal. His lavish home and headquarters, Hacienda Napoles, includes artificial lakes, an airport, and a house that can sleep 100 guests. He built a zoo at his residence that houses camels, lions, giraffes, bison, and llamas. Over the main gate he exhibits the small plane in which he flew his first cargo of illegal cocaine.

Jorge Ochoa is head of a family that has operated both in Colombia and the United States. It is said that he sent his younger brother to Miami, "to learn the family business," and to establish the Ochoas' dominance of the trade there.

Rodriguez Gacha is thought to control the cocaine distribution routes to the West Coast of the United States, through Los Angeles. Drug enforcement officials report that he became a major member of the cartel when he invested money with Escobar and the Ochoas to establish a huge jungle laboratory for processing cocaine.

Carlos Lehder has always been regarded as the most flamboyant of the top members of the cartel. Of the four major figures, he is the only one said to have used cocaine personally. He spent some of his early years in the U.S., where he was, by his own account, a "hippie." U.S. records show he was arrested in 1973 for marijuana possession and interstate car theft. He spent two years in a U.S. prison before returning to Colombia in 1975 to enter the cocaine trade. He purchased an island in the Bahamas, evicted its inhabitants, and established the area as a cocaine station through which 2,200 pounds of cocaine a month passed en route to the United States. With his profits, Lehder built a lavish hacienda that featured a nude statue of John Lennon, complete with a bullet hole through the heart.

Colombia's drug traffickers flaunted their wealth. They invested in legitimate businesses, set up new cocaine laboratory complexes, planted thousands of acres of coca bushes inside Colombia, and built grand haciendas for themselves. Several cocaine traffickers bought soccer teams. They also spread their wealth among the people. Some personally distributed cash among the poor on the streets of Medellin. Escobar built a roller-skating rink for the children of the barrio in which he had grown up. His company, Medellin Without Shanties, constructed a low-income housing project called Barrio Pablo Escobar.

The cocaine wealth attracted those who thought they could prey on the traffickers. Members of a leftist guerrilla movement called M-19 began to kidnap the relatives of the drug lords in Colombia, holding them for ransom. When the sister of Jorge Ochoa was kidnapped from the university she attended, the Ochoa family called a meeting of 230 major Colombian traffickers. Forming a group called MAS (Muerte a Secuestradores, "Death to Kidnappers"), they put together a $7.5 million fund to combat kidnappers. Airplanes showered a Colombian city with leaflets describing in detail punishments of death for members of M-19 or "their comrades in jail and . . . their closest family members." MAS made good on its threat. According to police, MAS members or its hired hands killed 100 people before Ochoa's sister was released unharmed.

This cooperative action was the real beginning of what became known as the Medellin Cartel. After 1981, the major Colombian dealers began to act in concert. They were no longer a collection of warring gangsters, but an organization that wielded enormous power.

Efforts to Capture the Cartel's Leaders

In 1979, the Colombian government agreed to honor a treaty that would allow Colombian violators of U.S. drug laws to be extradited and put on trial in the United States. The Medellin

A drug laboratory in Tranquilandia, Colombia, bursts into flames during the government's 1984 raid. Narcotics officers found and destroyed $1.2 billion worth of cocaine during this operation.

Cartel fought the treaty in all the ways that its wealth permitted. Both Lehder and Escobar started newspapers that insisted that the extradition treaty was "gringo" infringement on Colombian sovereignty. Escobar contributed heavily to a political party and was subsequently elected as an alternate member of the national legislature. Lehder founded a political party with a neo-Nazi orientation.

These ostensibly patriotic objections to the treaty carried weight with some Colombian politicians, apparently including newly elected president Belisario Betancur. When the extradition of Carlos Lehder was approved, Betancur held off signing papers necessary for the criminal's deportation. However, the country's new minister of justice, Rodrigo Lara, proved to be zealous in his desire to wipe out drug trafficking in Colombia. He drew up indictments against some of the major traffickers for violations of Colombian laws. Escobar and Lehder were forced to go into hiding. Then in 1984, Colombian police dealt the Medellin Cartel one of its severest blows.

In the southern part of Colombia the cartel had opened a huge cocaine laboratory complex, complete with airstrip and housing for workers. The Tranquilandia laboratories were producing and shipping 7,000 pounds of cocaine a month, and it was said they could more than double that output if necessary. However, in March 1984, Colombian narcotics police led by Colonel Jaime Ramirez found and destroyed the laboratory complex. They flushed 13.8 metric tons of cocaine (valued at $1.2 billion) down the Yari River.

The Colombian police also found that many of the workers in the complex were members of the FARC, a Spanish acronym for Colombian Revolutionary Armed Forces, a Marx-

The first Colombian nationals ever extradited to the United States arrive at the federal courthouse in Miami early in 1985. The two were charged with smuggling cocaine into the United States.

ist group. The FARC had been cooperating with the cartel for a percentage of its profits. News that cocaine profits were partially financing revolutionaries renewed the support of the nation's politicians for the antidrug crusade.

Six weeks later, the cartel struck back. Gunmen on motorscooters ambushed Justice Minister Lara's car, and assassinated him. The murder shocked the nation. President Bentancur called the traffickers "enemies of humanity" and declared a state of seige. He signed an extradition order for Lehder.

Lehder, Ochoa, Escobar, and some associates fled to Panama. There they arranged a meeting with ex-Colombian president Alfonso Lopez and denied having anything to do with the Lara assassination. On May 26, 1984, the trio met with Colombia's attorney general Carlos Jimenez, and made a spectacular offer. The cartel members admitted to controlling 70 to 80% of the cocaine produced in Colombia, a trade they valued at $2 billion yearly. They offered to disband their illegal activities, withdraw their funds from overseas banks and deposit the monies in Colombian banks, and cooperate in crop substitution projects and rehabilitation programs for Colombian addicts. In return, they asked for amnesty and exemption from the extradition treaty.

However, the U.S. government gave no credence to this offer, and began to increase its pressure on the cartel. It apprehended Barry Seal, an American pilot for the cartel's smuggling operation, and turned him into an informer. U.S. authorities sent him to pick up a planeload of cocaine being shipped from Nicaragua. A camera on the plane was used to take pictures of Escobar at the loading site.

Eventually, Escobar was indicted for the Lara assassination. The United States also obtained indictments against Ochoa and Rodriguez Gacha. Police in Spain arrested Ochoa, who had a lavish villa near Madrid, and the United States applied to Spain for his extradition. Colombia's new justice minister cooperated in processing extradition orders against others in the cartel. Colombia's police continued to seize record amounts of cocaine.

Faced with these difficulties, and getting nowhere with their offer, the cartel resumed its campaign of violence. On November 21, 1984, it issued a threat to kill five Americans for every Colombian extradited to the U.S. A car bomb outside the U.S. embassy in Bogota was the first evidence that this threat would be carried out. The car bomb killed a passerby and shattered windows in a three-block area. U.S. ambassador Lewis Tambs, who had been active in the effort to extradite the traffickers, was also targeted for assassination. After the cartel attempted to bribe the embassy's Colombian security personnel, Tambs left the country. All American dependents of embassy officials in Colombia were sent home as well. The DEA closed its offices in Medellin and Cali. The threat was taken so seriously that the DEA placed a police sniper on the roof of its headquarters in Miami. Nevertheless, despite the cartel's terrorist tactics, four Colombian traffickers were extradited to the United States in January 1985.

The Cartel Strikes Back

A series of assassinations followed in the wake of the arrests made by the Colombian government. The judge who had indicted Escobar was shot 13 times by 5 gunmen. Motor-scooter killers shot a Bogota prison warden who had blocked an escape attempt by a cartel member scheduled for extradition. This criminal eventually walked out of jail after spreading $2 million in bribes among his jailers.

The cartel's most spectacular exploit took place on November 5, 1985. A group of M-19 rebels financed by the cartel invaded Colombia's Palace of Justice, a meeting place for the country's Supreme Court. They held the building for 28 hours, killed 11 Supreme Court justices, and destroyed files relating to the cocaine trade. Tanks and soldiers were called in to retake the building, and in the ensuing violent melee 95 people died.

Meanwhile, U.S. efforts to extradite cartel leader Ochoa from Spain were thwarted when a Medellin judge sent the Spanish courts an extradition order that superseded the U.S. request. Ochoa was sent back to Medellin, charged with smuggling bulls, and released on $11,500 bail. He had eluded U.S. authorities once again.

Records of drug-related deaths continued to mount. Barry Seal, the American pilot who had obtained evidence against Escobar, was machine-gunned in Baton Rouge, Louisiana. Four Colombians were captured and found guilty of the murder in 1987. In Colombia, officials of Avianca Airlines

— which had begun to seize shipments of cocaine — were killed by motorscooter assassins. The editor of a Colombian newspaper that had crusaded against drugs was ambushed and killed. On November 17, 1986, Jaime Rodriguez, the former Colombian narcotics police chief who had destroyed the Tranquilandia lab, was killed in front of his wife and sons.

The following day, U.S. prosecuting attorneys in south Florida released a detailed indictment of the drug-related crimes allegedly committed by Escobar, Lehder, the Ochoa family, and Rodriguez Gacha. A month later, a Colombian newspaper published articles detailing the U.S. charges. The paper's editor was killed.

The cartel attempted to show the world that it could reach anywhere to harm those people and organizations opposing it. Former Colombian justice minister Enrique Parejo Gonzalez, a major cartel foe, had been sent as ambassador to Hungary for his own safety. On January 12, 1987, a gunman met him in Budapest and shot him five times. He survived, but the message was clear.

Four thousand journalists hold a silent demonstration in Bogotá, Colombia, for a colleague who was assassinated by drug traffickers in retaliation for his efforts to expose their operations.

Security was tight at the federal courthouse in Tampa, Florida, when drug cartel leader Carlos Lehder faced drug smuggling charges in 1987.

"One Down, Three to Go"

Antidrug forces reacting to this murderous onslaught scored a major coup on February 4, 1987, when one of the four Medellin kingpins was finally apprehended. A contingent of Colombian police acting on a tip surrounded a ranch house near Medellin. They captured 15 men, among them Carlos Lehder.

Lehder was swiftly extradited to Florida, where he was indicted on 11 counts of drug smuggling. Security precautions at his court appearances were extraordinary. People entering the Miami courtroom passed through metal detectors, and bomb-sniffing dogs roamed the corridors of the federal building. Parking on streets adjacent to the court was banned. The media reported that Lehder would be shifted to a number of secret locations while he awaited trial. Prosecuting officials charge that Lehder is a leader in a cartel that imported 58 tons of cocaine into the United States. If convicted, he will face a sentence of life imprisonment with no parole.

U.S. attorney Leon Kellner in Miami said of Lehder's capture, "One down, three to go." But even if the other Medellin Cartel leaders were arrested, the cocaine trade would not stop. Other eager dealers would quickly present themselves as substitutes, ready to handle the trade.

While the courage displayed by the antidrug forces may harm the international trafficking operations, there is little doubt that this industry will continue to thrive despite the antidrug victories, as long as demand for cocaine is high. Customs Service officials estimate that 137.5 tons of cocaine entered the United States in 1986. The U.S. Drug Enforcement Administration estimates that the Medellin Cartel handles up to 80% of this cocaine trade. A DEA agent in Colombia described the antidrug war as "stepping on a half-inflated balloon. Air bubbles just slide out the edges of your foot."

U.S. Attorney General Edwin Meese (right) examines a haul of marijuana confiscated by federal agents in Arkansas. Some estimates claim that marijuana is the third most valuable cash crop in the United States.

CHAPTER 4

MARIJUANA AND OTHER DRUGS

Marijuana is the most commonly used illegal drug. The marijuana plant, or *Cannabis sativa*, grows in many areas throughout the world. The spindly plant's leaves, stems, and seeds are smoked in cigarette form. A more concentrated form of marijuana can be obtained in the resin of the mature flower. This potent substance is called hashish.

Marijuana is different from heroin and cocaine in that it does not need to be chemically processed to be ingested. People can simply harvest a small crop for local and almost immediate consumption. As a result, marijuana is not only imported from other countries, but is produced within the United States in substantial quantities by professionals and amateurs alike. Users believe that certain countries produce better varieties of marijuana and are willing to pay a premium for imported types. However, the bulk of the product makes large-scale smuggling cumbersome.

Because marijuana is commonly available and usually not cut many times as heroin or cocaine is, the profits to be made by growing and selling this substance are proportionately lower than for other drugs. But high demand continues to ensure that marijuana dealing is still a very lucrative business.

National Guard helicopters are used in police raids on remote marijuana patches on Kauai, Hawaii.

The general belief that marijuana is not as harmful as other drugs and a relaxation of legal penalties for possession have led to its wide use among various segments of society.

Sinsemilla, a seedless type of marijuana with much higher levels of the plant's psychoactive ingredient, THC, has also become a popular crop among both growers and users. Common marijuana has 1 to 1.5% THC; sinsemilla may have as high as 12 to 13%. A single sinsemilla plant can produce $1,000 worth of marijuana.

Marijuana Production in the United States

The DEA estimates that U.S. production of marijuana was 2,100 metric tons in both 1985 and 1986. During this time, it was grown mostly in California, Oregon, and Hawaii (although it was found in all 50 states). Some estimates claim that marijuana is the nation's third most valuable cash crop, worth in excess of $10 billion a year. The depressed economy in many rural areas has caused some farmers to plant marijuana crops. The sheriff of Washington County, Iowa, remarked, "If you put out one acre of marijuana, you can make more than on your entire farm operation. Think about that."

Many of the marijuana growers in California operate in the "Emerald Triangle," which includes most of Humboldt, Trinity, and Mendocino counties in the northern part of the state. Approximately 1.5 million acres of heavily forested public land comprises a large portion of the triangle. Until recently, growers operating in this region were not bothered by law enforcement authorities. However, in the wake of incidents where campers and other visitors to the national forests were shot at or injured by booby traps set by the growers, officials have been alerted to illegal activity in the region. (A favorite device was a trip wire at ankle level, attached to a hand grenade.)

The U.S. Department of Agriculture, which operates the National Forest Service, allocated $20 million to root out marijuana growing in the "Emerald Triangle" and in other parts of the nation's forest system. California set up a program called Campaign Against Marijuana Planters (CAMP) that used helicopters and planes to spot the crops. Then local sheriffs and Forest Service agents raided the marijuana plantations. The program has been successful in eradicating large amounts of marijuana; 166,219 plants were destroyed in 1985. However, California officials have been less successful in prosecuting the growers themselves. Of 1,100 growers arrested in 1984, only ten went to prison.

Public acceptance of marijuana continues to undermine efforts to eradicate its cultivation and consumption. Although marijuana use among high school students is reported to have dropped in recent years, some statistics say that as many as one-third of Americans occasionally smoke it. A 1982 *Newsweek* poll showed that 40% of Americans thought that growing marijuana for personal use should not be a criminal offense.

In Hawaii, where a program similar to California's CAMP was tried, the prosecutor of Hawaii County commented, "We've caught people with a couple of tons of marijuana, but the courts don't look on that as a serious crime. We've sent maybe three people to prison in the last six years." The sheriff of Mendocino County, California, said, "I think that taxpayers are 2-to-1 against marijuana, but they'd rather see their tax dollars spent elsewhere."

Foreign Sources of Marijuana

The United States government has maintained diplomatic and economic pressure on foreign countries to discourage marijuana growing within their borders. Most of the marijuana imported into the United States comes from Mexico. Provinces in the central part of the country produce large supplies of marijuana, which has long been used by Mexicans. Those farmers now growing it claim that marijuana brings far greater profits than ordinary food crops.

From the mountains of such provinces as Guerrero, baled marijuana is brought down on the backs of mules to Mexican cities such as Caihuacan and Tijuana, where the drug culture thrives. In Tijuana City, just across the border from southern California, dealers hire specialists to carve hiding places in vehicles for marijuana smuggling. Then the drug is carried across the U.S. borders by illegal immigrants, tourists, or members of Mexican criminal syndicates that have branches across the border.

Under pressure from the United States, the Mexican government agreed to try to exterminate its marijuana crop. Helicopters were employed to spray plants with the poisonous chemical paraquat. To thwart this effort, some growers camouflaged their plants in remote fields alongside other tall plants such as corn. However, the Mexican government is continuing to cooperate with the United States in marijuana eradication programs.

Colombia is second only to Mexico in marijuana production. Marijuana from Colombia is smuggled into the United States in much the same way as cocaine; planes and ships are used to carry illegal cargoes. Sometimes, the drug is smuggled into Mexico and then taken into the United States by trucks, campers, or boats. Americans involved in the trade can take boats from any of the marinas on the California coast and cruise to a Mexican port, pick up Colombian or Mexican marijuana, and return home. Legally, a person is supposed to notify authorities when crossing an international border, but smugglers have found ways to circumvent this procedure. The California coast has many marinas where boats can easily dock, and in truth, the Coast Guard cannot possibly patrol the whole area.

Jamaica and Belize are also major suppliers of marijuana to the United States. In Jamaica, "ganja" (marijuana) smoking is widespread and accepted. Cultivation of this crop is a $1.1 billion business and provides more revenue than all other exports combined. Nevertheless, Jamaica's prime minister, Edward Seaga, is, according to the U.S. State Department, "firmly committed to the eradication and interdiction [of marijuana]." The U.S. government allocated $2.6 million in 1986 and 1987 to help the Jamaican eradication effort.

Nonetheless, the program is opposed by nearly half of all Jamaicans, according to one poll. As with the cocaine barons of Colombia, Jamaica's drug traffickers have assumed

A Mexican soldier burns marijuana plants. Under immense pressure from the United States, the Mexican government has agreed to try to eradicate the country's marijuana crops.

A coffee shop in Amsterdam uses a marijuana leaf to announce that the drug is for sale inside. City authorities in Holland permit the use of marijuana and hashish in coffeehouses.

a Robin Hood posture. They have built schools and roads and provided families with food. Some Jamaicans question whether or not their country could afford to lose its marijuana revenues.

In response to pressure from the United States, the government of Belize has also adopted an aerial-spraying program to eliminate marijuana. However, cultivation of the plant on this island more than doubled in 1986.

Marijuana in Europe

Marijuana use is widespread in most European countries, including the Soviet Union. The Christiana district of Copenhagen, Denmark is one of the biggest marijuana markets in the world. Buyers come from all parts of Europe to purchase drugs there, which they resell at home. In Amsterdam, Holland, city authorities permit the use of marijuana and hashish in coffeehouses. (However, in 1987, Dutch police drew the line when a courier service advertised free home delivery of marijuana and hashish.) Spain decriminalized possession of the drug in 1983.

Much of the marijuana sold in Europe is grown in Africa. Ghana and Nigeria are major producers. Dealers in these countries transport marijuana cargoes to European nations by sea and air.

Hashish

Hashish, a substance with a high THC content that is derived from marijuana, is produced mainly in the countries of the Middle East and Afghanistan. The drug has long enjoyed popularity in these regions. The center of the hashish trade is in Lebanon, in the Bekaa Valley around the town of Baalbak. Hashish produced in this region is sent to other Middle Eastern countries, Europe, and the United States. The civil war in Lebanon has curtailed the activities of hashish traders only

A farmer from the Bekáa Valley in Lebanon carries his fall crop of freshly dried hashish to a nearby market.

slightly. But the American market for hashish has shrunken somewhat lately, partly because regular marijuana is now so strong that many people see no reason to buy the more expensive, harder-to-get hashish.

Synthetic Drugs

In addition to heroin, cocaine, and marijuana, a considerable number of synthetic (or man-made) drugs are abused in the United States and elsewhere each year. Many of these drugs — including amphetamines, narcotics, and tranquilizers — are produced by pharmaceutical companies for legitimate medical purposes. However, misuse of prescription drugs is notorious. Many people have become addicted to the painkillers or barbiturates prescribed by their doctors. Still others obtain various pharmaceutical preparations on the black market, a source of such drugs in which the supply is generated through

A professor discusses the chemical structure of methyl fentanyl, a heroinlike substance. There is a thriving black market for synthetic drugs, which are often stolen from pharmaceutical companies or hospitals.

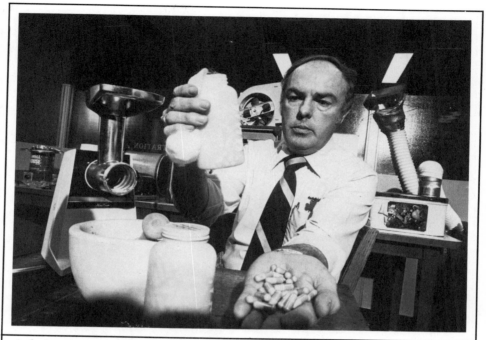

A federal agent displays chemicals and equipment seized during a 1976 raid on a methaqualone laboratory in Pittsburgh. This compound is no longer manufactured legally, but illicit production continues.

direct theft or diversion from hospitals, drugstores, and pharmaceutical companies. Many Mexican pharmacies in Tijuana participate in these illegal operations.

In Europe, the centers of the synthetic drug trade are Sweden and Denmark. Sweden has a severe problem with drugs, particularly amphetamines. When the Swedish government acted to limit legal sources of amphetamines in the 1960s, illegal laboratories began to appear to supply the large demand.

One synthetic drug that can only be obtained through illegal means is PCP, commonly known as "angel dust." PCP has produced violent reactions among its users when taken alone or combined with marijuana and smoked. Congress passed the Psychotropic Substances Act of 1978, which imposed penalties for the manufacture or possession of such chemicals.

Two Hell's Angels after a narcotics raid in California. The Hell's Angels have become a major source for illegal prescription drugs.

Chemists in private laboratories also produce what are called "designer drugs." These are synthetic drugs that are chemically similar to the illicit drug on which they are modeled. Designer drugs produce much the same effects as illicit psychoactive drugs but are not technically illegal since their contents have not been thoroughly analyzed and classified. Nonetheless, the United States government has begun to target some designer drugs and add them to the prohibited list.

Another synthetic drug that continues to play a part in the illicit drug trade is LSD. First synthesized in 1938, LSD became popular among college students in the 1960s. Unfortunately, after a period of eclipse, the drug is now reappearing on high school and college campuses. Just a minute amount of LSD is needed for a high, so it can easily be concealed. Like any synthetic drug, it can be produced wherever the chemical knowledge is available. LSD laboratories have been found in most European cities and in the United States. And once again, people not ordinarily thought of as criminals have been caught making and selling LSD. For example, the head of New York University's Anthropology Department was found guilty of dealing in LSD in 1980.

Quaaludes, a trade name for methaqualone, are commonly sold on the streets. They were originally introduced as a prescription sedative. However, quaaludes quickly became widely abused, and their manufacture was consequently banned. Nonetheless, in the early 1980s, American cities were awash in bootleg "ludes." The DEA traced them to Colombia and with the help of the South American government closed the laboratories. But as found in other segments of the drug trade, when one lab or route is policed, another opens in a different location. Today, laboratories in East Asia are the source of illegal methaqualone tablets, which are easily smuggled into the country because of their small and manageable size. "Ludes" are still available in many parts of the United States and Europe.

The Hell's Angels have become a major source for illegal prescription drugs. Originally a motorcycle gang, the group has branched out to dealing in drugs of all kinds. They operate throughout the United States and Canada, taking advantage of the unpoliced border between the two countries. From such Canadian cities as Montreal, they also carry heroin into the United States.

A money launderer testifies before a congressional committee. In 1986 Congress made money laundering a federal crime, hoping to thwart drug dealers' efforts to hide their enormous stores of cash.

CHAPTER 5

THE ILLEGAL MONEY CHAIN

The drug business is conducted on a strictly cash-and-carry basis. Credit is rarely available and checks are never used. Thus, drug traders accumulate enormous sums of cash that cannot be declared on tax returns or deposited in banks without arousing suspicion. There is a need to "launder" this money — that is, transfer it into legitimate financial channels or shelters.

Dealers tied to large drug operations often turn their money over to professional money launderers. For a small percentage, often only one or two percent of the total, drug money launderers will use a variety of means to turn the "dirty" money into cleaner "legal" money. Until 1986, money laundering was not a crime in itself; however, that year Congress passed a new law that made the practice a federal crime.

How Money Launderers Operate

Before 1986 the principal weapon against drug launderers was a provision of the 1970 Bank Secrecy Act, which required financial institutions to report deposits and withdrawals of cash in excess of $10,000 to the Treasury Department. Exceptions were made for certain legal businesses, such as supermarkets, that commonly deal in large amounts of cash. Legalized gambling casinos in Nevada and New Jersey were also exempted from this provision. Consequently, the Mafia, which had ties to some Nevada casinos, used these establishments to launder illegal money obtained from all sorts of activities, including drug sales.

In the early 1980s, the case of Humberto and Eduardo Orozco revealed the enormity of this problem. On October 5, 1981, Humberto Orozco brought 233 pounds of currency into the Manhattan offices of the Deak-Perera currency exchange. The amount of the deposit totaled over $3,400,000. Two days later, Orozco reappeared with cash that was only a $20 bill short of $1 million. The following day, he deposited more than $500,000. Five days later, he deposited $879,000 and three days after that $1,476,420. Such huge sums — all in cash — might have been expected to attract attention. As banking authorities say, however, their job is not to catch criminals. Deak-Perera complied with the law and filed the required forms with the U.S. Treasury Department. Thousands of banks and other financial institutions file similar reports every day.

In fact, these sums represented only a small fraction of the money the Orozco brothers were putting into New York financial institutions. During a four-year period, they deposited approximately $151 million in cash in various banks and currency exchanges such as Deak-Perera.

What happened to the reports that Deak-Perera and the banks made about the Orozcos' large cash deposits? Unfortunately, the volume of such reports is great. Since international banks maintain a Clearance House Interbank Payment System (CHIPS) that allows them to transfer funds electronically, instead of actually moving the cash, banks around the world transfer some $220 billion *every day*. Officials of the Treasury Department have trouble processing all the transfer reports they receive each day. The Orozcos were confident that they could carry on their business without interference — particularly because money laundering was not a crime in the early 1980s. Federal authorities estimate that there were and still are thousands of launderers with similar operations.

In fact, the Orozcos were caught only because an attorney working for the brothers realized that drug proceeds from Colombian cocaine dealers and Sicilian heroin traffickers made up the bulk of their cash holdings. He tipped off

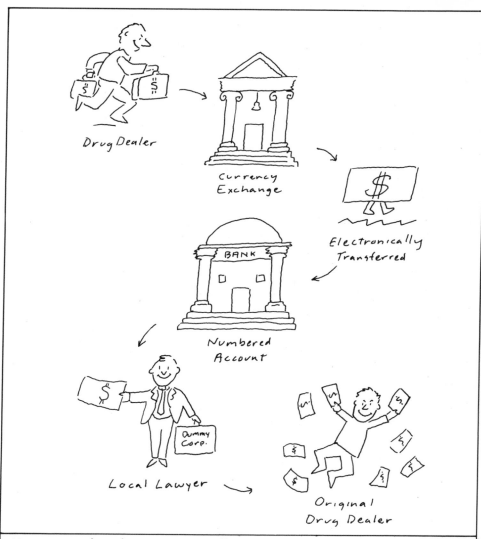

How money launderers operate: Illegal funds are deposited with a currency exchange, which transfers them to a numbered bank account. Then a lawyer representing a dummy corporation borrows the funds and "loans" them back to the original source — namely, the drug dealer.

the Drug Enforcement Administration, which set up a "sting" operation that employed a DEA agent posing as a bank official. The agent wore a tape recorder during discussions with Eduardo Orozco and obtained evidence that eventually got the Orozcos convicted on charges of conspiring to violate the drug laws.

A collage of Swiss bank nameplates. Switzerland has signed a mutual legal assistance treaty with the United States and is taking steps to rid its banks of drug money.

Overseas Money Laundering Centers

The next step in the laundering process is to transfer the money to bank accounts in one of several countries that have strict bank secrecy laws. (In recent years, many nations have imitated Switzerland, which remains the nation most famous for instituting and zealously protecting a nondisclosure policy in its financial community.) It is possible to open a numbered account that protects the identity of the depositor. A "dummy" corporation that exists only on paper is then set up to protect and "legitimatize" the account. The Cayman Islands in the Caribbean had in 1983 some 13,600 registered corporations — nearly one for every resident of the islands. And in Panama, another major laundering center, more than 200,000 of these corporations are on record.

A local lawyer handling the affairs of a dummy corporation may withdraw money from the account and "loan" it to the original source of the money, in this case, the drug dealer. The dealer can then claim it legally, and use it for any purpose. As one money launderer explained the process, "You're going to take (the money) out of your right-hand pocket and pay it back into your left-hand pocket ... You haven't transported money out of the United States, which is a crime. You haven't taken a risk of carrying it, and it's done on a bank-to-bank basis." Countries that have bank secrecy laws also protect corporations from being investigated by foreign sources. U.S. officials are often unable to prove that the money in these accounts comes from illegal activities.

Currently, the U.S. government is making a major effort to persuade countries with money-laundering banks to cooperate in attempts to identify sources of the funds. The Antidrug Abuse Act of 1986 includes a provision requiring the U.S. State Department to identify countries with bank secrecy laws. In the case of those countries that receive U.S. aid, financial assistance may be cut off if they do not agree to a mutual legal assistance treaty.

Swiss banks continue to be the hub for money-laundering operations in Europe. However, Switzerland has signed a mutual legal assistance treaty with the United States and is taking steps to rid its banks of drug money. The Swiss government has frozen and forfeited several million dollars in drug proceeds since the treaty went into effect.

According to the State Department, Great Britain has "several banking institutions [that] are utilized by various groups to conceal their illicit drug profits. London banks, for example, receive a portion of the profits generated by Mideastern heroin and hashish traffickers." Britain has also agreed to release banking information to U.S. authorities under certain legal guidelines.

Panama has become the largest money-laundering center for U.S. drug dealers. The fact that U.S. currency is legal tender in Panama makes the country an attractive haven for illicit profits. Under pressure from the United States, Panama passed a narcotics control law in December 1986 that makes laundering of drug money a criminal offense. However, Panama's banks, which have thrived with the influx of money created by Panama's bank secrecy laws, are resisting efforts to change the system. Some people fear that Panama's new law may be intended only as a concession to U.S. pressure and will not be seriously enforced.

As we have seen, influxes of drug money into secret bank accounts have helped the Cayman Islands become a significant international banking center. There are over 500 banks in the small Caribbean nation. However, agreements in 1984 and 1986 between the United States and Britain — which maintains some political control over the Cayman Islands, a former colony — gave the United States access to records of accounts set up in the island where criminal involvement is suspected and can be proven.

The Bahamas, another country in the Caribbean, has a banking situation similar to the one that exists in Panama. Though this country also passed drug-laundering legislation, the State Department concluded in 1987 that "the Bahamas continues to play a major role in the laundering of narcotics funds."

Financial Institutions in the United States

The United States must also look at domestic banks that may be helping criminals protect or profit from drug-related cash deposits. Banks have been lax or late in reporting major cash transactions. In some cases, bank officials have been part of laundering operations. In February 1985, for example, the Bank of Boston was convicted of cooperating in a money-laundering scheme. After the case received wide publicity, banks were more conscientious about reporting currency transactions; the number of such reports filed with the Treasury Department quadrupled. The Treasury Department nonetheless penalized more than two dozen financial institutions between 1985 and 1987 for failure to report properly. The Crocker National Bank was fined $2.25 million for failing to report $3.4 billion in domestic and international cash deposits and withdrawals. In January 1986, the Bank of America was fined $4.75 million for failing to report more than 17,000 cash transactions.

In Miami, the so-called cocaine capital of the United States, the number of new banks mushroomed during the 1970s and 1980s. There is so much cash going into southern Florida's banks that at one point the Miami branch of the

Federal Reserve reported a cash reserve greater than that in the rest of the country's banks combined. Depositors with paper bags or suitcases stuffed with cash were common sights in Miami banks. Tellers complained that the money smelled as if it had been buried. Often, this was the case. Depositors usually had no trouble getting their money accepted by the banks; indeed, some of these financial institutions are owned by drug traders themselves.

Fueled by drug money, Miami has become a banking center for Latin America. Sting operations have caught such money launderers as Isaac Kattan, a Colombian who is thought to have laundered $5 million weekly for Colombian drug traffickers. He was sentenced to 30 years in prison.

Bankers have said that it is not really their job to investigate their customers. U.S. attorney Rudolph Giuliani disagrees: "I've heard some bankers complain that it's not their role to act as detectives. . . . It is my view that they are wrong

Once money has been laundered, it becomes available for investment in legitimate businesses. Criminals are attracted to video arcades and other operations that routinely take in large amounts of cash.

Depositors lined up outside Miami's failed Sunshine State Bank in 1986, hoping to get their money back. A marijuana smuggler has been accused of buying the bank in 1978 with illegal drug profits.

as a matter of law and as a matter of sound business judgment. The law places responsibility on banks to obtain and report [information] concerning domestic and foreign transactions ... irrespective of legal ramifications, any bank that allows itself to be used as a conduit for drug money is in danger of severely damaging its image and reputation for prudence and integrity. At the same time, it is exposing its employees, who have to deal with many sensitive situations, to being tempted to involve themselves in crime."

Profits from the Drug Trade

Once money has been laundered, it becomes available for investment in legitimate businesses. But the people who control these funds are still criminals, and they often corrupt the businesses they invest in as well. The Mafia has long been active in buying into certain kinds of business. Its control of parts of the construction industry in New York City has helped to drive up building costs in that city. South American, Asian, and European drug traders have followed the Mafia's lead. Typically, criminals prefer to invest in those businesses that commonly deal in cash purchases, such as car washes, check-cashing outlets, video-game arcades, fast-food chains, jewelry stores, and boutiques. The potentially lucrative real estate industry has become another outlet for "dirty" money.

Drug criminals may even occasionally purchase banks both in the United States and abroad. Control of a bank obviously makes the money-laundering task that much easier and criminals are aware of which banks may be ripe for a laundering operation. The Senate Banking Committee, in fact, has put together a list of 21 Miami banks that handled suspected drug money and/or systematically underreported cash transactions to the Treasury. A Miami banker stated, "You wouldn't believe how many people come in here to ask if the bank is for sale."

A businessman from Medellin, Colombia, bought the Bank of Perrine in Miami, Florida, in 1981. He was later jailed and his assets seized by the Colombian government in connection with bank fraud in that country. Florida banking officials discovered the businessman had concealed his criminal record on the application he had filed to purchase the Bank of Perrine. Duplicity and concealment were that easy. And no doubt, the businessman's case is not unique. The danger of organized criminals' control of large amounts of cash is that they can buy into, and then corrupt, legitimate businesses as well.

A New York City police officer is led to his arraignment on charges of selling drugs confiscated from local dealers. Corruption of law enforcement officials is a scourge of illicit drug trafficking.

CHAPTER 6

THE CRIME OF CORRUPTION

For society, one of the most serious drug-related crimes is corruption. This corruption includes the tainting of political officials, law-enforcement officers, and members of the judiciary. In many of the countries that grow opium and cocaine, the per capita income is very low. Drug dealers can offer bribes that are far greater than any ordinary person can make from legitimate work. In the case of some poor Latin American and Asian countries, the income from the drug trade surpasses the profit from any other exported goods.

Corruption in Producer Countries

In Bolivia, the coca leaf is the country's single most important export. Drug traffickers routinely bribe officials at all levels of the government and the army. Salaries of government officials and army officers are so low that this money is eagerly accepted. In addition, law-enforcement officials often must face the credible threat that they will be killed if they actively oppose the drug trade. When faced with the option of taking a bribe or being targeted for assassination, most officials choose the seemingly wiser course.

Many livelihoods are tied to the drug trade in under-developed countries. Often, it is not possible to stop the flow of drug-related money without creating a backlash. Roberto Suarez has allegedly become one of the most important men in Bolivia as a result of his control of the coca leaf-growing areas. His wealth was so great that when President Carter cut off aid to Bolivia in protest against that country's lax drug policy, Suarez was able to make up the difference.

After a coup toppled Bolivia's government in 1980, the drug traffickers actually became the government. Santa Cruz traffickers paid General Luis Garcia Meza over a million dollars to stage the coup. After taking power, General Meza named Roberto Suarez's cousin and cohort as his minister of the interior. A reign of terror followed. Many honest officials were killed and all records of drug trafficking were destroyed. For more than a year, the Bolivian army and the national airline were at the disposal of the drug trade. Finally, a civilian

Mexican president Miguel de la Madrid (right) presents the Aztec Eagle, Mexico's highest honor, to Alan Garcia, the president of Peru. De la Madrid has launched a "moral renovation" campaign in Mexico in an effort to stamp out the official corruption his predecessor, Jose Lopez Portillo, called "the cancer of this country."

government was returned to office in 1982. As noted in Chapter 3, this new government cooperated with U.S. efforts to eradicate Bolivian coca plantations and cocaine exportation. The new president's antidrug policies drove General Meza and two leading figures of the drug business into exile in Argentina. However, Roberto Suarez, protected by his multibillion dollar business, was untouched by these reforms. He remains the reported head of the cocaine trade in Bolivia.

Bolivia is an extreme, but not isolated, example of corruption on a national level. A similar situation exists in Colombia. Politicians are "bought" with drug money. Those officials not willing to cooperate are threatened. Judges are given the choice of taking bribes or bullets. The *Miami Herald* quoted one Colombian judge as saying, "You can take the $50,000 and let the defendant go. Or you can die." Most judges make the rational, if unethical, choice, for officials who are willing to protect drug traffickers find themselves rewarded with fantastic amounts of money.

In Mexico, drug-related corruption has affected all levels of society. The police are particularly susceptible. Bribes offered for "looking the other way" equal more than a year's salary ($2,400) for a police officer. Government officials are also among those accepting bribes.

Ten years ago, shortly before his inauguration, Mexican president Jose Lopez Portillo said, "Corruption is the cancer of this country." During his six-year term, official efforts were made to stamp it out. Nevertheless, several people who held high office during his term were prosecuted for bribery by the succeeding government, headed by Miguel de la Madrid. Samuel I. Del Villar, a professor at the Collegio de Mexico in Mexico City, was once chief adviser for President de la Madrid's "moral renovation" campaign, but resigned. He says in retrospect, "What worried me is the velocity [with which] corruption is accelerating through the government. It's the most serious threat to national security we face. If the government doesn't do something about it, it will destroy our country." He added, "I have watched the most distinguished police commanders, the best the federal police had in the 1970s, inevitably become corrupted. If you move the army into drug enforcement, inevitably they will be corrupted too. It's impossible to resist, especially in these times of economic crisis."

Relations between the United States and Mexico have been strained by the drug issue. A particularly bitter incident occurred when a DEA agent was killed in Mexico in 1985, with the complicity of the Mexican police. Members of the U.S. Congress have been particularly vehement in denouncing Mexico's government since the murder. Mexicans, on the other hand, resent what they see as U.S. interference in their affairs. The new American ambassador to Mexico in 1987 took a conciliatory tone, pointing out that some 400 Mexican soldiers and narcotics agents have also been killed in the fight against drug traffickers in recent years.

A rise in opium production in Laos, a communist country, has also been attributed to government cooperation. According to the *Washington Post*, Western drug enforcement officials "have often suggested privately that the Laotian government was directly involved in the opium trade." The paper also quoted an adviser to the Thai prime minister as saying that "It was Laotian state enterprises themselves that were organizing [the growing of opium poppies]." Western officials note that the Laotian government is strapped for cash and relies on the opium trade as one of its few major exports.

The body of DEA agent Enrique Camerena, who was tortured to death by drug traffickers in Mexico in 1985, is returned to the United States.

Military strongman General Manuel Noriega, commander-in- chief of Panama's National Defense Forces, has been linked in many published accounts with drug trafficking, money laundering, and other illegal activities.

Corruption in Transit Countries

The Bahamas remain a transit point for cocaine and marijuana destined for the United States. Trafficking in this area is so prevalent that U.S. authorities doubt it could be carried on without the cooperation of high government officials. In 1984, a special commission in the Bahamas documented corruption throughout the government, and cited members of the cabinet. After the report was issued, five cabinet ministers were replaced by Prime Minister Sir Lynden Pindling. Pindling, who was also regarded with suspicion by members of the U.S. government, said in 1986 that "one can never dispel" anxiety about corruption. "There have been and may still be corrupt people in a number of places," he said.

In Panama, the situation threatens to erupt in much the same way as it did earlier in Bolivia. General Manuel Antonio Noriega, the effective ruler of the country for several years, has been linked to drug trafficking, money laundering, and other illegal activities. He has also ordered the dismissal of five presidents in five years.

When Colombia's drug barons had to flee their country, they found a haven in Panama. Panama's banks are known as the major conduits for drug money laundering. In June 1986 the *New York Times* reported that law-enforcement officials in the Nixon administration proposed to assassinate General Noriega to help curb Panama's drug traffic. Yet, because Panama is the location of the vital Panama Canal, the United States has been helpless to put effective economic pressure on the nation and its corrupt government.

Corruption in the United States

There is no evidence that major officials of the federal government have been corrupted in the United States. Most of the corruption in this country has been among various local law-enforcement officials. Although these employees are not as poorly paid as their counterparts in Mexico, they cannot claim to make anything like the money that filters through the hands of drug traders. Coast Guard officers have reportedly been offered bribes of up to $15,000. Some people have fallen for the trafficker's bait. A secretary working for the DEA in Florida was sent to jail for stealing secret intelligence files. Police forces in Boston, Los Angeles, Miami, and New York have had major scandals. There have also been cases of local government officials being caught dealing in drugs.

In 1972, heroin that had been confiscated in the so-called French Connection case was reported missing from the New York Police Department stolen property office. It had been kept, rather than destroyed, to be used as evidence if the Frenchmen who escaped were caught. A major portion of heroin that had been confiscated in various other drug cases in the 1960s was also missing. An ensuing investigation uncovered massive corruption in the department's Special Investigation Unit. Ironically, this unit had originally been established to catch major drug dealers. Members of this elite corps had taken money from drug dealers and apparently sold the missing heroin to organized crime members who distributed it. Following this discovery, the unit was disbanded and New York City police were no longer involved in drugs except at the local level. Major drug investigations were left to federal agencies.

In the 1980s, corruption in one police precinct in New York City had reached the point where some police officers were actually dealing in drugs themselves. They were accused of selling drugs that they had confiscated from street dealers. New York's police commissioner set up a system of rotating assignments to prevent such a situation from recurring. Although thousands of New York police officers protested his action, claiming that it impugned the integrity of the entire force, some radical reform was clearly in order.

Bribery and corruption have become rampant in those regions of the country — chief among them southern Florida — through which drugs are imported. Half of an entire division of the Dade County police force was indicted for payoffs and drug trafficking. Federal officials are not immune to bribes and favors. A former group supervisor of the DEA's Miami offices was indicted in 1982 by a federal grand jury on smuggling and corruption charges. Jack Rafferty, the chief of narcotics investigation for Dade County, Florida, said, "The money floating around has the potential to corrupt nearly anyone."

An elderly woman is led to an ambulance after being mugged on a New York City subway platform. An overwhelming percentage of street crimes are committed by abusers of illicit drugs.

CHAPTER 7

DRUGS AND STREET CRIME

The crimes that average Americans most commonly fear are potentially violent street crimes — robberies, muggings, and burglaries. Because illegal drugs are expensive, users frequently resort to theft to support their habits. Murder, as we have seen, is a routine part of the drug trade.

The level of street crimes in the United States and Europe has risen in recent years, and so have incidences of drug abuse. Many law-enforcement officials say the two statistics are related. A number of studies have shown that drug use among those arrested for crimes is much higher than among the general population.

The Connection Between Drug Use and Street Crime

In 1986, a study of crime in Manhattan showed that 78% of men arrested for serious crimes were also cocaine users. This compared with a statistic of 42% recorded in a similar study in 1984. The commander of the New York Police Department's Narcotics Division said, "There's no question [that] there is a close correlation between the recent increase we've experienced in violent crime, and the increase this study has shown in the use of drugs."

Governor Mario Cuomo addressed an anticrack rally to inaugurate New York's "Crack down on Crack" campaign in 1986.

Researchers at Temple University in Philadelphia completed a study in 1980 that found a connection between heroin dependence and street crime in an American city. Their report said that 243 addicts studied were responsible for having committed more than 500,000 crimes in Baltimore, Maryland, over an 11-year period. The study followed the addicts during times when they were "on" and "off" drugs. During the times when they were off drugs, these individuals committed 84% fewer crimes than when they were using drugs.

During the mid-1980s, the number of murders in most American cities rose drastically. Nine of the 10 largest American cities showed a significant rise in murders between 1985 and 1986. During the same period, the number of people arrested in federal drug cases rose from 15,695 to 18,746. Drug suspects arrested by state and local police dropped to around 550,000 in 1979, and then rose to over 700,000 in 1984. Was there a connection between the rise in murders and the rise in drug arrests? Many officials believe that a connection can be found. They theorize that the popularity of drugs such as cocaine and crack can be tied directly to increasing rates of violence. The chief homicide detective in Oakland, California, said, "We wouldn't have a murder problem if it weren't for drugs."

European countries have also seen an increase in the crime rate as drugs have become more available. Some European experts have claimed that drug users are responsible for up to 50% of crimes, such as robberies, committed by juveniles or young adults.

The Effect of Crack

The appearance of crack on city streets in the United States in the early 1980s seemed to trigger a rise in crime statistics. This rise followed a relatively stable period in the 1970s when crime rates declined. Crack is a crystalline form of cocaine that is smoked rather than snorted. It is made by heating cocaine with other materials, such as baking soda.

Authorities say that crack — usually sold in small vials costing around $10 — produces a short but intense high. The high is followed by a craving for more of the drug.

Crack first appeared in Los Angeles, Miami, Houston, and Detroit; by 1986, according to the operators of a hotline for drug abusers, use of the drug had spread to 17 major cities around the country. Some cocaine dealers discovered they could make crack easily in home labs and thereby multiply their profits. *Newsweek* magazine reported the story of a crack dealer named "Eare." He began as a street seller of angel dust, and then invested $1,600 in an ounce of cocaine. He turned this drug into crack by mixing it with other chemical elements and sold the new drug in small lots for a profit of $6,000. Now he has 12 to 15 runners who sell the crack for him; Eare clears $12,000 a week.

Because crack is relatively new and can be manufactured on a small scale, the trade has been controlled by individuals or small groups at the local level. Police trace the increase in juvenile gang violence in such cities as Detroit and Los Angeles to the gangs' involvement with crack sales. A spokesman for the Los Angeles police department said the rise in homicides in that city resulted from "territorial disputes among gangs who all want the privilege of selling cocaine." Moreover, innocent bystanders have been killed by gangs fighting each other for turf.

U.S. Attorney Rudolph Giuliani unfurls the arrest record of a crack dealer who has been arrested 27 times in 10 years. The justice system is strained almost to the limit by the volume of cases generated by drug-related offenses.

Ever-Younger Victims

One of the most alarming developments on the contemporary drug scene is the increasing numbers of very young people who are using — and selling — drugs. Grade-school children are now being introduced to glue sniffing, marijuana, and crack. Hunter Hurst, director of the National Center for Juvenile Justice, says, "Drug use used to be a decision of adolescence. Now it's a fourth-grade decision."

Among this age group, crimes of all kinds have risen as well. Between 1978 and 1983, referrals to juvenile courts nationwide rose 37% for 13-year-olds, 38% for 12-year-olds, 22% for 11-year-olds, and 15% for 10-year-olds. James A. Payne, chief of New York's family court, confirmed that drug use was one reason for the rise in crimes committed by very young children. "Crack is the main reason," Payne said. "We are seeing kids as young as 10 or 11 [as crack dealers]. They can make $800 a week. They only stay in school because that's where their constituency is."

As drugs become more prevalent in society as a whole, they filter down to the very young. Some young users were raised in households where their parents or other adults were drug users. Judge Tom Rickhoff of San Antonio says, "I see more and more children of parents who are mentally ill or on drugs." Other children have been drawn into drug use by dealers who wanted to use them as couriers and sellers. In a 1987 New Jersey case, girls of 11 and 12 were hooked on crack by two women who then forced them to have sex with men to "earn" additional crack.

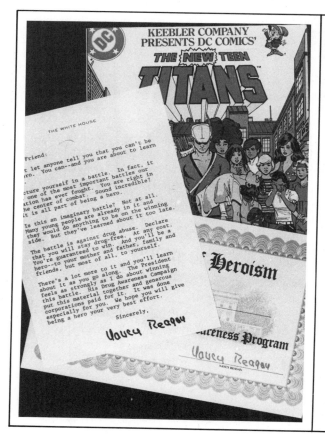

A sampling of antidrug materials distributed by the Department of Education to about one million fourth graders in 35,000 schools.

In 1987 the New York City police created a special force that has significantly reduced the volume of flagrant drug trafficking in Washington Square Park, long known as a "drug supermarket."

The Efforts of Local Communities

The federal government has repeatedly attempted to keep drugs from entering the country or to cut the supplies of drugs at their source. Getting drugs off the streets of the nation's towns and cities has become a top priority of local governments. Communities around the country have tried a variety of measures to eliminate the street trade in drugs.

People who live in communities plagued by drugs constantly call for increasing the numbers of police on the street. In Washington, D.C., in 1986, the police department instituted Operation Clean Sweep to get drugs off the streets of the nation's capital. In the first six months of the program, police confiscated $6.8 million in drugs and made over 6,000 arrests on drugs charges. Most of the drug arrests were for PCP.

Washington Square Park in New York has long been known as a "drug supermarket." Located in fashionable Greenwich Village and bordered by New York University, the park has attracted marijuana and crack dealers who openly hawk their wares. In early 1987, police assigned a large task force to the park. Members of the force were equipped with dogs trained to sniff out drugs. The police commissioner said that 2,700 arrests had been made in the area over the previous 15 months, but admitted that the problem still existed. When police began arresting buyers as well as sellers of drugs in the park, area residents noticed an immediate lull in illicit trafficking.

The practice of arresting the drug buyer, however, was largely abandoned by police in the 1960s and 1970s when it became apparent that drug experimentation was too prevalent to arrest all of society's users. Unfortunately, arresting street dealers has proven equally futile in the 1980s. Even when a dealer goes to jail, others soon step in to take his place.

The Reagan administration has recently called for renewed efforts to concentrate "on the demand side." Some cities have resumed a policy of arresting drug buyers. In

Residents decorated this Harlem tenement with stuffed animals and murals in an effort to call attention to New York City's war on crack.

Washington Heights, an area of Manhattan close to the George Washington Bridge, drug dealers have flourished because users from New Jersey drive across the bridge to buy drugs. The surrounding neighborhood became a well-known market for cocaine and then crack. In 1986, the New York police began arresting buyers in the Washington Heights area and impounding their cars. Among those arrested were doctors, lawyers, and a New Jersey police officer. New York police seized 420 cars in the first 6 months of the program. A crack dealer who said that he had made $1,000 a night before the crackdown said he was now making only $100.

The Failure of the Justice System

Police saturation of certain areas often halts a drug trafficking problem for a short time. However, the resources of police departments are limited, and such intense coverage of a single area cannot be maintained indefinitely. Although drug dealers

New York City's mayor Edward Koch (center), U.S. Attorney Rudolph Guiliani (second from right), and other officials pose with a car that was impounded when its driver was arrested while buying drugs.

can be driven out of a neighborhood, they soon set up shop elsewhere. Moreover, both the court system and the prisons are clogged with drug offenders; many arrested dealers serve short terms in jail or are simply fined or placed on probation for their crimes.

In the face of increasing numbers of drug arrests, prosecutors and judges have had to accept plea-bargaining as one way of processing all the cases presented to them. Typically, a person charged with a crime agrees to plead guilty to a lesser charge in return for a lenient sentence which may not even involve time in jail. To try each case before a jury on the original charge would bring the justice system to a halt, because there are not enough judges or prosecutors to handle jury trials that may take days or weeks. For example, in New York City in 1985, there were 55,000 arrests for drug violations; only 3,000 of them resulted in jail terms of more than 30 days for the offender. Drug dealers are well aware of these statistics, and often regard arrest as merely a risk involved in doing business.

Some politicians and government officials have called for mandatory jail terms for drug dealers. New York State tried that in 1973. Under the prodding of Governor Nelson Rockefeller, the state made the mandatory punishment for dealing drugs a life term. Studies showed that juries were reluctant to convict minor dealers, knowing that the penalty was life imprisonment, and eventually the mandatory life penalty was repealed.

If even half of the individuals arrested on drug charges were sentenced to jail, there would not be enough cells to accommodate them in the prison system. The New York City correctional system is now at 104% of capacity. The Los Angeles County Jail holds 20,000 inmates in a facility meant for 11,000. Past court cases have shown that prisoners can successfully appeal for relief from such overcrowded conditions. Yet taxpayers have proved reluctant to vote for the building of additional jail space.

Local Neighborhoods Fight Back

It is obvious that the street crimes associated with drug dealing strongly affect those who live in the neighborhoods where drugs are sold. Fights between drug dealers for control of

A Tampa, Florida, advertisement urges citizens to turn in local "pushers." Across the country, private citizens are banding together to protest widespread drug abuse and its tragic consequences.

turf can and do kill innocent bystanders. Drug dealers will sell to anyone with money, including children. People also rightly fear the effect drug dealers flaunting their wealth will have on a neighborhood's young people.

In the past, it was taken for granted that drugs were sold only in poor neighborhoods. Then, as now, these areas are the least likely to receive full-scale police protection. In the 1980s, however, drug dealing is a common sight on suburban playgrounds and in fashionable urban areas. In retaliation, residents everywhere — poor and middle-class alike — are taking bold steps to reclaim the streets for themselves and their children.

On Kennedy Street in an area of Washington, D.C., just four miles north of the Capitol building, a cocaine market operated openly for many years. Business people and residents of the area finally banded together to demand increased police surveillance. In a four-year battle for their rights, the residents began to see results. By 1987, new businesses began moving onto Kennedy Street. Currently, the area is thriving. Jesse Brown, owner of a local barber shop, is a member of the Advisory Neighborhood Commission that helped drive the Kennedy Street dealers out. "We are a close neighborhood, and we took control of the problem," Brown says.

Thurman Smith, the president of the Ditmas Area Coalition in a neighborhood of Brooklyn, New York, has also mobilized his community to combat drug dealers. "We have a bad drug problem in this area," Smith says. "We've held marches, we've picketed, we've complained to the police in the 70th precinct here. So now we're going to do it our way."

Smith charges that the police neglect the Ditmas area because mostly poor people live there. But with the help of residents, Smith has compiled his own list of local drug dealers. He threatens to bring charges against them in court and has petitioned the housing court to evict them from their public housing. For his own protection, Smith carries a baseball bat. To some, these moves suggest vigilante action. But to many people living in areas plagued by the drug epidemic, taking matters into their own hands seems to be the only way they can protect themselves.

Conclusion

The manufacture, distribution, and consumption of illicit drugs are inexorably linked to crime. A vicious cycle of supply and demand governs the drug trade, one of the most lucrative businesses in the world today. Experience shows that even the most zealous efforts by law-enforcement officials to wipe out the supply only drives those who traffic in drugs to ever-escalating tactics of evasion and violence. So long as individuals — teenagers looking for marijuana, Wall Street executives willing to pay any price for cocaine, Hollywood hotshots toying with heroin — continue to create a market for drugs, so long will the unscrupulous merchants who dominate this market continue to flourish.

APPENDIX

State Agencies for the Prevention and Treatment of Drug Abuse

ALABAMA
Department of Mental Health
Division of Mental Illness and
  Substance Abuse Community
  Programs
200 Interstate Park Drive
P.O. Box 3710
Montgomery, AL 36193
(205) 271-9253

ALASKA
Department of Health and Social
  Services
Office of Alcoholism and Drug
  Abuse
Pouch H-05-F
Juneau, AK 99811
(907) 586-6201

ARIZONA
Department of Health Services
Division of Behavioral Health
  Services
Bureau of Community Services
Alcohol Abuse and Alcoholism
  Section
2500 East Van Buren
Phoenix, AZ 85008
(602) 255-1238

Department of Health Services
Division of Behavioral Health
  Services
Bureau of Community Services
Drug Abuse Section
2500 East Van Buren
Phoenix, AZ 85008
(602) 255-1240

ARKANSAS
Department of Human Services
Office of Alcohol and Drug Abuse
  Prevention
1515 West 7th Avenue
Suite 310
Little Rock, AR 72202
(501) 371-2603

CALIFORNIA
Department of Alcohol and Drug
  Abuse
111 Capitol Mall
Sacramento, CA 95814
(916) 445-1940

COLORADO
Department of Health
Alcohol and Drug Abuse Division
4210 East 11th Avenue
Denver, CO 80220
(303) 320-6137

CONNECTICUT
Alcohol and Drug Abuse
  Commission
999 Asylum Avenue
3rd Floor
Hartford, CT 06105
(203) 566-4145

DELAWARE
Division of Mental Health
Bureau of Alcoholism and Drug
  Abuse
1901 North Dupont Highway
Newcastle, DE 19720
(302) 421-6101

DISTRICT OF COLUMBIA
Department of Human Services
Office of Health Planning and
  Development
601 Indiana Avenue, NW
Suite 500
Washington, D.C. 20004
(202) 724-5641

FLORIDA
Department of Health and
  Rehabilitative Services
Alcoholic Rehabilitation Program
1317 Winewood Boulevard
Room 187A
Tallahassee, FL 32301
(904) 488-0396

Department of Health and
  Rehabilitative Services
Drug Abuse Program
1317 Winewood Boulevard
Building 6, Room 155
Tallahassee, FL 32301
(904) 488-0900

GEORGIA
Department of Human Resources
Division of Mental Health and
  Mental Retardation
Alcohol and Drug Section
618 Ponce De Leon Avenue, NE
Atlanta, GA 30365-2101
(404) 894-4785

HAWAII
Department of Health
Mental Health Division
Alcohol and Drug Abuse Branch
1250 Punch Bowl Street
P.O. Box 3378
Honolulu, HI 96801
(808) 548-4280

IDAHO
Department of Health and Welfare
Bureau of Preventive Medicine
Substance Abuse Section
450 West State
Boise, ID 83720
(208) 334-4368

ILLINOIS
Department of Mental Health and
  Developmental Disabilities
Division of Alcoholism
160 North La Salle Street
Room 1500
Chicago, IL 60601
(312) 793-2907

Illinois Dangerous Drugs
  Commission
300 North State Street
Suite 1500
Chicago, IL 60610
(312) 822-9860

INDIANA
Department of Mental Health
Division of Addiction Services
429 North Pennsylvania Street
Indianapolis, IN 46204
(317) 232-7816

IOWA
Department of Substance Abuse
505 5th Avenue
Insurance Exchange Building
Suite 202
Des Moines, IA 50319
(515) 281-3641

KANSAS
Department of Social Rehabilitation
Alcohol and Drug Abuse Services
2700 West 6th Street
Biddle Building
Topeka, KS 66606
(913) 296-3925

KENTUCKY
Cabinet for Human Resources
Department of Health Services
Substance Abuse Branch
275 East Main Street
Frankfort, KY 40601
(502) 564-2880

LOUISIANA
Department of Health and Human
    Resources
Office of Mental Health and
    Substance Abuse
655 North 5th Street
P.O. Box 4049
Baton Rouge, LA 70821
(504) 342-2565

MAINE
Department of Human Services
Office of Alcoholism and Drug
    Abuse Prevention
Bureau of Rehabilitation
32 Winthrop Street
Augusta, ME 04330
(207) 289-2781

MARYLAND
Alcoholism Control Administration
201 West Preston Street
Fourth Floor
Baltimore, MD 21201
(301) 383-2977

State Health Department
Drug Abuse Administration
201 West Preston Street
Baltimore, MD 21201
(301) 383-3312

MASSACHUSETTS
Department of Public Health
Division of Alcoholism
755 Boylston Street
Sixth Floor
Boston, MA 02116
(617) 727-1960

Department of Public Health
Division of Drug Rehabilitation
600 Washington Street
Boston, MA 02114
(617) 727-8617

MICHIGAN
Department of Public Health
Office of Substance Abuse Services
3500 North Logan Street
P.O. Box 30035
Lansing, MI 48909
(517) 373-8603

MINNESOTA
Department of Public Welfare
Chemical Dependency Program
    Division
Centennial Building
658 Cedar Street
4th Floor
Saint Paul, MN 55155
(612) 296-4614

MISSISSIPPI
Department of Mental Health
Division of Alcohol and Drug Abuse
1102 Robert E. Lee Building
Jackson, MS 39201
(601) 359-1297

MISSOURI
Department of Mental Health
Division of Alcoholism and Drug
    Abuse
2002 Missouri Boulevard
P.O. Box 687
Jefferson City, MO 65102
(314) 751-4942

MONTANA
Department of Institutions
Alcohol and Drug Abuse Division
1539 11th Avenue
Helena, MT 59620
(406) 449-2827

NEBRASKA
Department of Public Institutions
Division of Alcoholism and Drug
Abuse
801 West Van Dorn Street
P.O. Box 94728
Lincoln, NB 68509
(402) 471-2851, Ext. 415

NEVADA
Department of Human Resources
Bureau of Alcohol and Drug Abuse
505 East King Street
Carson City, NV 89710
(702) 885-4790

NEW HAMPSHIRE
Department of Health and Welfare
Office of Alcohol and Drug Abuse
   Prevention
Hazen Drive
Health and Welfare Building
Concord, NH 03301
(603) 271-4627

NEW JERSEY
Department of Health
Division of Alcoholism
129 East Hanover Street CN 362
Trenton, NJ 08625
(609) 292-8949

Department of Health
Division of Narcotic and Drug
   Abuse Control
129 East Hanover Street CN 362
Trenton, NJ 08625
(609) 292-8949

NEW MEXICO
Health and Environment Department
Behavioral Services Division
Substance Abuse Bureau
725 Saint Michaels Drive
P.O. Box 968
Santa Fe, NM 87503
(505) 984-0020, Ext. 304

NEW YORK
Division of Alcoholism and Alcohol
   Abuse
194 Washington Avenue
Albany, NY 12210
(518) 474-5417

Division of Substance Abuse
   Services
Executive Park South
Box 8200
Albany, NY 12203
(518) 457-7629

NORTH CAROLINA
Department of Human Resources
Division of Mental Health, Mental
   Retardation and Substance Abuse
   Services
Alcohol and Drug Abuse Services
325 North Salisbury Street
Albemarle Building
Raleigh, NC 27611
(919) 733-4670

NORTH DAKOTA
Department of Human Services
Division of Alcoholism and Drug
   Abuse
State Capitol Building
Bismarck, ND 58505
(701) 224-2767

OHIO
Department of Health
Division of Alcoholism
246 North High Street
P.O. Box 118
Columbus, OH 43216
(614) 466-3543

Department of Mental Health
Bureau of Drug Abuse
65 South Front Street
Columbus, OH 43215
(614) 466-9023

OKLAHOMA
Department of Mental Health
Alcohol and Drug Programs
4545 North Lincoln Boulevard
Suite 100 East Terrace
P.O. Box 53277
Oklahoma City, OK 73152
(405) 521-0044

OREGON
Department of Human Resources
Mental Health Division
Office of Programs for Alcohol and
  Drug Problems
2575 Bittern Street, NE
Salem, OR 97310
(503) 378-2163

PENNSYLVANIA
Department of Health
Office of Drug and Alcohol
  Programs
Commonwealth and Forster Avenues
Health and Welfare Building
P.O. Box 90
Harrisburg, PA 17108
(717) 787-9857

RHODE ISLAND
Department of Mental Health,
  Mental Retardation and Hospitals
Division of Substance Abuse
Substance Abuse Administration
  Building
Cranston, RI 02920
(401) 464-2091

SOUTH CAROLINA
Commission on Alcohol and Drug
  Abuse
3700 Forest Drive
Columbia, SC 29204
(803) 758-2521

SOUTH DAKOTA
Department of Health
Division of Alcohol and Drug Abuse
523 East Capitol, Joe Foss Building
Pierre, SD 57501
(605) 773-4806

TENNESSEE
Department of Mental Health and
  Mental Retardation
Alcohol and Drug Abuse Services
505 Deaderick Street
James K. Polk Building,
  Fourth Floor
Nashville, TN 37219
(615) 741-1921

TEXAS
Commission on Alcoholism
809 Sam Houston State Office
  Building
Austin, TX 78701
(512) 475-2577
Department of Community Affairs
Drug Abuse Prevention Division
2015 South Interstate Highway 35
P.O. Box 13166
Austin, TX 78711
(512) 443-4100

UTAH
Department of Social Services
Division of Alcoholism and Drugs
150 West North Temple
Suite 350
P.O. Box 2500
Salt Lake City, UT 84110
(801) 533-6532

VERMONT
Agency of Human Services
Department of Social and
  Rehabilitation Services
Alcohol and Drug Abuse Division
103 South Main Street
Waterbury, VT 05676
(802) 241-2170

APPENDIX: STATE AGENCIES

VIRGINIA
Department of Mental Health and
Mental Retardation
Division of Substance Abuse
109 Governor Street
P.O. Box 1797
Richmond, VA 23214
(804) 786-5313

WASHINGTON
Department of Social and Health
Service
Bureau of Alcohol and Substance
Abuse
Office Building—44 W
Olympia, WA 98504
(206) 753-5866

WEST VIRGINIA
Department of Health
Office of Behavioral Health Services
Division on Alcoholism and Drug
Abuse
1800 Washington Street East
Building 3 Room 451
Charleston, WV 25305
(304) 348-2276

WISCONSIN
Department of Health and Social
Services
Division of Community Services
Bureau of Community Programs
Alcohol and Other Drug Abuse
Program Office
1 West Wilson Street
P.O. Box 7851
Madison, WI 53707
(608) 266-2717

WYOMING
Alcohol and Drug Abuse Programs
Hathaway Building
Cheyenne, WY 82002
(307) 777-7115, Ext. 7118

GUAM
Mental Health & Substance Abuse
Agency
P.O. Box 20999
Guam 96921

PUERTO RICO
Department of Addiction Control
Services
Alcohol Abuse Programs
P.O. Box B-Y Rio Piedras Station
Rio Piedras, PR 00928
(809) 763-5014

Department of Addiction Control
Services
Drug Abuse Programs
P.O. Box B-Y Rio Piedras Station
Rio Piedras, PR 00928
(809) 764-8140

VIRGIN ISLANDS
Division of Mental Health,
Alcoholism & Drug Dependency
Services
P.O. Box 7329
Saint Thomas, Virgin Islands 00801
(809) 774-7265

AMERICAN SAMOA
LBJ Tropical Medical Center
Department of Mental Health Clinic
Pago Pago, American Samoa 96799

TRUST TERRITORIES
Director of Health Services
Office of the High Commissioner
Saipan, Trust Territories 96950

Further Reading

Bakalar, James B., and Lester Grinspoon. *Drug Control in a Free Society*. Cambridge: Cambridge University Press, 1984.

Brecher, Edward M., and the editors of *Consumer Reports. Licit and Illicit Drugs*. Boston: Little, Brown, 1972.

Daley, Robert. *Prince of the City*. New York: Houghton Mifflin, 1978.

Dolan, Edward F., Jr. *International Drug Traffic*. New York: Franklin Watts, 1985.

Freemantle, Brian. *The Fix*. New York: Tor Books, 1986.

Greenhaw, Wayne. *Flying High*. New York: Dodd, Mead, 1984.

Grinspoon, Lester. *Marijuana Reconsidered*. Cambridge: Harvard University Press, 1977.

Grinspoon, Lester, and Peter Hedblom. *The Speed Culture*. Cambridge: Harvard University Press, 1975.

Illegal Drugs and Alcohol: America's Anguish. Plano, TX: Information Aids, 1985

Jones, Helen C., and Paul W. Lovinger. *The Marijuana Question*. New York: Dodd, Mead, 1985.

Lernoux, Penny. *In Banks We Trust*. Garden City, NY: Doubleday, 1984.

Louria, Donald B. *The Drug Scene*. New York: McGraw-Hill, 1968.

McCoy, Alfred W. *The Politics of Heroin in Southeast Asia*. New York: Harper & Row, 1972.

Mills, James. *The Underground Empire*. Garden City, NY: Doubleday, 1986.

Phillips, Joel L., and Ronald D. Wynne. *Cocaine: The Mystique and the Reality*. New York: Avon Books, 1980.

Traub, James. *The Billion Dollar Connection*. New York: Julian Messner, 1982.

Trebach, Arnold S. *The Heroin Solution*. New Haven: Yale University Press, 1982.

U.S. Department of State. Bureau of International Narcotics Matters. *International Narcotics Control Strategy Report*. Washington, D.C.: GPO, March 1987.

Glossary

addiction a condition caused by repeated drug use characterized by a compulsive urge to continue using, the drug, a tendency to increase the dosage, and physiological and/or psychological dependence

Anti–Drug Abuse Act of 1986 U.S. federal law that requires the State Department to identify countries that are not taking steps to halt the growing, manufacturing, or trafficking of drugs that are illegal in the United States

Bank Secrecy Act of 1970 U.S. federal law that requires financial institutions to report deposits and withdrawals of cash in excess of $10,000 to the Treasury Department

bank secrecy laws laws that protect the identity of bank depositors; countries with such laws make it difficult for other nations' law enforcement officials to trace the source of illegal money that has been laundered

beat generation a group of writers and artists of the 1950s who advocated rebellion against society and were called "beats"

black market illegal trade in prescription drugs, especially those that produce a desirable effect

Campaign Against Marijuana Planters (CAMP); California state program employed in the mid-1980s to stamp out marijuana growing

coca bush plant grown in South America; its leaves are processed to make cocaine

cocaine the primary psychoactive ingredient in the coca plant and a behavioral stimulant

commission a loose federation of Mafia families organized in 1931 to prevent disputes over territory between the families

contrabandistas professional smugglers who fly contraband or illegal goods from the United States to South American countries and return with cargoes of illegal drugs

Controlled Substances Act U.S. federal law passed in 1970 that made possession of small quantities of marijuana a misdemeanor, rather than a felony

crack a crystalline preparation of cocaine, usually smoked

designer drugs synthetic drugs with a chemical structure similar to such illegal drugs as cocaine; they produce a similar high but are not illegal because they are not identical to the illegal drugs they mimic

Drug Enforcement Agency (DEA) U.S. federal agency formed in 1973 by combining former drug agencies in various cabinet departments into one central agency

dummy corporation a corporation that exists only on paper and may serve as a temporary holding place for illegal drug money that is being laundered

Eighteenth Amendment amendment to the U.S. Constitution that prohibited the manufacture and sale of alcoholic beverages; ratified in 1919, it was repealed by the Twenty-first Amendment in 1933

emerald triangle part of California, including most of Humboldt, Trinity, and Mendocino counties that contains most of California's marijuana production

extradition treaty a treaty between two countries that permits a criminal accused or convicted of a crime in one country to be returned there by another country

Federal Bureau of Narcotics U.S. federal government agency within the Treasury Department; created in 1932 to enforce the antidrug laws

French Connection heroin manufacturing and distribution network centered in Marseilles, France

ganja Jamaican term for marijuana

Golden Crescent major opium producing area in western Asia where Pakistan, Iran, and Afghanistan adjoin

Golden Triangle major opium producing area of Southeast Asia where Burma, Laos, and Thailand meet

Hague Conference of 1912 international conference at which major nations of the world met and agreed to restrict the production and trade of opiates to the amount needed for medicinal purposes

Harrison Narcotics Act of 1914 U.S. federal law that requires anyone who imports, manufactures, or sells narcotics to register with the government and pay a special tax

hashish a psychoactive substance made from the dried and pressed flowers and leaves of the hemp plant; it contains a high concentration of THC, the active ingredient in the plant

heroin a semisynthetic opiate produced by a chemical modification of morphine

high the sudden feeling of well-being, pleasure, or relaxation that certain drugs initially induce in the user

hooked addicted to drugs

LSD lysergic acid diethylamide; a hallucinogen derived from a fungus that grows on rye or from morning glory seeds

marijuana a psychoactive substance with the active ingredient THC found in the crushed leaves, flowers, and branches of the hemp plant

MAS (Muerte a Secuestradores "Death to Kidnappers") a group of Colombian drug traffickers formed to combat kidnappings of their family members; predecessor of the Medellin Cartel

Medellin Cartel a loose organization of Colombian cocaine manufacturers and distributors whose headquarters are in or near the city of Medellin, Colombia

methadone a drug that has been legally administered to heroin addicts to help them break their addiction; it is addictive and is available in most countries by prescription only

milieu French underworld organization based in Marseilles; its members are predominantly Corsicans

money laundering a financial process by which illegal profits from the drug trade are secretly transferred so that they appear to be legitimate sources of income

morphine an opiate used as a sedative and pain reliever

mule a person who carries illegal drugs, primarily cocaine, on his or her body through customs

M-19 Colombian leftist guerrilla group associated with the cocaine trade

narcotic originally a group of drugs producing effects similar to morphine; often used to refer to any substance that sedates, has a depressant effect, and/or causes dependence

paraquat a chemical that poisons the marijuana plant; it is sprayed from planes or helicopters by government antidrug programs

PCP also called phencyclidine; an illicit drug used for its stimulating, depressing, and/or hallucinogenic effects

physical dependence adaption of the body to the presence of a drug such that its absence produces withdrawal symptoms

pizza connection heroin distribution network consisting of Sicilian Mafia members who operated through pizza parlors in the eastern half of the United States

psychological dependence a condition in which the drug user craves a drug to maintain a sense of well-being and feels discomfort when deprived of it

Psychotropic Substances Act of 1978 U.S. Federal law that imposes penalties for the manufacturing or possession of synthetic drugs such as PCP that produce hallucinogenic effects and feelings of euphoria or disorientation

Pure Food and Drug Act of 1906 U.S. federal law that required labels on all medicines to clearly state the alcohol, narcotic (heroin), and cocaine content

Quaaludes trade name for methaqualone, a prescription drug used as a sedative; illegal methaqualone tablets are commonly sold in the street drug trade

shotgun a person employed by a drug organization who follows a "mule" to guarantee that the illegal drugs arrive and are delivered

sinsemilla a seedless type of marijuana with much higher levels of THC, the psychoactive ingredient

synthetic any drug that is produced in a laboratory and does not occur in nature

tolerance a decrease of susceptibility to the effects of a drug due to its continued administration, resulting in the user's need to increase the drug dosage to achieve the effects experienced previously

transit country a country through which drugs pass from production to market

withdrawal the physiological and psychological effects of discontinued usage of drugs

PICTURE CREDITS

Index

Polo, Marco, 25
President's Commission on Organized
    Crime, 20
Prohibition, 31
Psychotropic Substances Act (1978), 77
Pure Food and Drug Act (1906), 29

Quaaludes, 34, 79
Queens, 58

racism, 28
Rafferty, Jack, 97
Ramirez, Jaime, 62
Reagan, Ronald, 36, 105
Red Brigades, 46
Reefer Madness, 30
Rickhoff, Tom, 103
Ricord, Auguste, 40, 41
Rockefeller, Nelson, 107
Rodriguez, Jaime, 65

San Antonio, 103
San Francisco, 34
Santa Cruz, 52, 92
Seaga, Edward, 73
Seal, Barry, 63, 64
Senate Banking Committee, 89
Shan State Army, 42
Shining Path, 54
"shotguns," 56
Sicily, 45–48
Silicon Valley, 35
Singapore, 43
Sinoloa, 46
Smith, Thurman, 109

soldier's disease, 26
South Florida Task Force, 37
Soviet Union, 22, 44, 74
Spain, 75
State Department, U.S., 55, 73, 85, 86
Suarez, Roberto, 53, 54, 92, 93
Sweden, 77
Switzerland, 84, 85
synthetic drugs, 76–79
Syria, 39

Tambs, Lewis, 64
Temple University, 100
Thailand, 41–43, 94
Tijuana, 72, 77
Tinga Linda, 52
Tranquilandia laboratories, 62, 65
tranquilizers, 76
Treasury Department, U.S., 29, 31, 81, 82,
    86
Trinity County, 71
Turkey, 39–41, 44, 45, 47

Vietnam War, 33, 34, 43, 44
Vin Mariani, 27

Wall Street, 34, 109
Ward, Benjamin, 19
Washington, D.C., 104, 108
Washington Heights, 106
Washington Post, 42, 94
Washington Square Park, 104
World War II, 32, 40
Yari River, 62
Yugoslavia, 45

Dorothy and *Thomas Hoobler* live and work in New York City and are coauthors of more than 20 books. Among their recent titles for Chelsea House are *Zhou Enlai* and *Cleopatra.*

Solomon H. Snyder, M.D. is Distinguished Service Professor of Neuroscience, Pharmacology and Psychiatry at The Johns Hopkins University School of Medicine. He has served as president of the Society for Neuroscience and in 1978 received the Albert Lasker Award in Medical Research. He has authored *Uses of Marijuana, Madness and the Brain, The Troubled Mind, Biological Aspects of Mental Disorder,* and edited *Perspective in Neuropharmacology: A Tribute to Julius Axelrod.* Professor Snyder was a research associate with Dr. Axelrod at the National Institutes of Health.

Barry L. Jacobs, Ph.D., is currently a professor in the program of neuroscience at Princeton University. Professor Jacobs is author of *Serotonin Neurotransmission and Behavior* and *Hallucinogens: Neurochemical, Behavioral and Clinical Perspectives.* He has written many journal articles in the field of neuroscience and contributed numerous chapters to books on behavior and brain science. He has been a member of several panels of the National Institute of Mental Health.

Joann Ellison Rodgers, M.S. (Columbia), became Deputy Director of Public Affairs and Director of Media Relations for the Johns Hopkins Medical Institutions in Baltimore, Maryland, in 1984 after 18 years as an award-winning science journalist and widely read columnist for the Hearst newspapers.